GET OFF
THE COUCH–
SEE IT LIVE!

JEFFREY JACOBS

Experiencing the world's most prestigious
sporting events from a fan's perspective

Published & distributed by:
Jeffrey Jacobs

in association with:
IBJ Book Publishing, LLC
Indianapolis, IN
www.ibjbookpublishing.com

ISBN - 978-1-939550-55-2

Library of Congress Control Number: 2017934165

Table of Contents

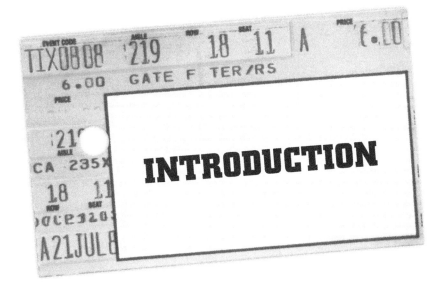

INTRODUCTION

Experiencing the world's most exciting, significant and prestigious sporting events became an interest of mine years ago. It's difficult to pinpoint, precisely, the catalyst for this quasi addicting behavior of being one of the ultimate sports spectators–given my rather underdeveloped athletic talents, I realized the closest I would get to playing a professional sport would be viewing it firsthand. And since my talents at academics and attracting the opposite sex were rather limited, too, I was focused, full speed ahead, on sports–viewing sporting events–LIVE.

Growing up, sports consumed me–reading, watching, learning and participating. From the age of eight years old, I read the sports pages, oftentimes twice a day. In the morning, I woke at 6:30, jumped out of bed, ran downstairs and sprinted to the end of the driveway to pick up the newspaper; specifically, the *Chicago Tribune's* sports section. I couldn't wait to read the latest scores of the Bears, Hawks, Bulls, Sox and Cubs—obsessed with learning what my local sports heroes had just done the day or night before—athletes such as Bobby Hull, Gale Sayers, Billy Williams and the list goes on. After my daily reading ritual, I would hand the then-read *Tribune's* sports section to my father, as he headed off to work by 7:30. Then in the evening, my father came home with the *Chicago Daily News,* returning the favor of handing me the sports section he had read on the train coming home. And for Christmas, I always asked to receive subscriptions to two sports magazines—*Sports Illustrated* and *Sport* magazine. Being pre-ESPN, these magazines were my only link to the national sports teams and national athletes and I read these publications voraciously, further sparking my interest in and love for sports.

Despite never having achieved any material success playing athletics, I did have the benefit of participating in three experiences that merit repeating and, in their own way, contributed to my passion for collegiate and professional athletics. And they each occurred at about the same age.

When I was 10, my father worked for the NBC radio station in Chicago—WMAQ, which, among other things, broadcasted the Chicago White Sox games. One year for our spring vacation, he took the family down to their spring training camp in Sarasota. As my sisters built sandcastles and swam in the ocean, collecting sea-shells, to my great surprise, my dad arranged for me to have a private hitting session with Eddie Stanky, the manager of the Sox, nicknamed "The Brat," in the batting cage. At 10 years old, I was shorter than five feet, weighing about 75 pounds, and using a major league bat—half the length of my body. It was an accomplishment to actually swing that piece of lumber, let alone make contact with the ball, traveling at 85 mph from the batting machine. Contact was actually achieved on the 22nd pitch (Stanky was counting)—a foul tip, of course. For over an hour, Manager Stanky provided me with batting advice that I will always remember—but never was enough to get me past Little League status (the advice was not faulty, just its execution.)

That same year, only a few months later, I was part of a situation that was truly remarkable on several fronts, and has been told hundreds of times. On this particular day, we were playing pick-up ball at a friend's house, running through the muddied field from a thunderstorm that morning. After playing for about an hour, we somehow lost our last baseball, before we completed the official nine innings.

None of us had an extra baseball. However, my friend, Sherman Reynolds, who was hosting the game, mentioned his father had a ball up in his closet. Well, naturally, we encouraged him to go inside and get the ball from his father's closet, as soon as possible—we had a game to finish.

He retrieved the ball and brought it down to the "field." However, this was a very unique baseball—it was signed by each of the four Beatles (this was 1966) and Hank Aaron. Well, as the saying goes "The show must go on"—Batter Up! So, for the next hour, on a muddy field, we played with a pretty valuable (not for long) baseball.

This story's ending is almost as unbelievable as the aforementioned details. The good news is we did not lose the ball. However, after having played with it in muddy conditions, the four Beatles and Hank Aaron's signatures could have been those of the Three Stooges—who could tell at that point? The combination of mud, grass, bat and general handling of the ball caused the ink to run and fade. Being the responsible son my friend was, after the game, he promptly returned the ball to his father's closet. Are you curious how this will play out?

Two weeks later, Sherman's father noticed the "altered" baseball and summoned his son to his room to determine culpability. Sherman openly admitted to using the ball with his friends. His father probed further and asked, "Did you all have fun?" The response: "Yes, Dad, we had a great time."

You now wonder: What was his father's response to this? Well, it was simple: "That's what's important son. I'm glad you had a great time." No screaming, no punishment, no repercussions–nothing. (In baseball jargon "Safe at Home!") Those would not be the words and reaction of my father–how about yours? Today, as we all get together and reminisce, we question the true value of the ball had it not been played by eight determined boys. At this point, it's moot. The real value has been telling the story and hearing how people react to both damaging such a valuable possession and seeing them react to the father's rather benevolent behavior to his damaged possession.

And then the following year, 1967, I attended my first golf tournament–The Western Open–not a major, but one that brought many of the top golfers to Chicago. Golf was not one of my favorite sports, by any stretch, but attending the tourney was once again eventful and fueled my desire to witness some of the world's most acclaimed sporting events.

On this day, I met and received an autograph from golf's greatest legend, Jack Nicklaus. That encounter, however, would pale in comparison to one of my most embarrassing moments at any public event, let alone a golf tournament.

My friend Sherman and I scooted from hole to hole, watching some of the world's greatest golfers. Then, with no planning on our part, we found ourselves watching a very young Ray Floyd, who would become a champion of numerous golf majors. On this particular hole, Mr. Floyd was about 70 yards from the pin. I happened to be right behind him as he was about to chip onto the green. After his final practice swing, as he was moments away from making his chip, I realized how close his club had come to hitting me. Concerned while he began his back swing, I moved to avoid being hit with his club!

Naturally, my movement disturbed him, causing Mr. Floyd to stop in the middle of his back swing. He rested the club on the ground, looked at me and said "Son, please don't move when a golfer is preparing to hit their ball." So, as he prepared to hit, once again, this time I remained motionless—holding my breath, until the complexion of my face was a different hue from my God-given pale—heeding his recent advice.

Well, fortunately, my distraction caused him to focus even harder on his shot, resulting in his chipping the ball about two feet from the cup. After making the obligatory "gimme" putt, he turned toward the gallery and asked, "Where is that boy who moved in the middle of my backswing?" Embarrassed, I covered my face with my handy program—to no avail. The gallery, interested in seeing how this interaction would play out, all pointed to me. Mr. Floyd promptly walked toward me, tossing me his ball (rather than throwing it at me) and said, "Son, let this be a reminder to be more considerate of golfers when you are on the golf course." I have since followed his advice religiously—except when money is involved with my golfing buddies.

So, in the following pages, what you will experience is a collection of stories I've accumulated over the last 35 years, attending some of the world's most noteworthy sporting events (according to my provincial perspective). It's my hope that this will not be seen as a brag "look what I have done" book, but will share some rather humorous (and sometimes eventful) anecdotes from the average spectator's view—my own.

Growing up, I dreamed of witnessing, LIVE, many of the

events I share with you in this book. Presumably, you, too, would like to attend (if you already haven't) some of the following athletic contests—clearly, the best seat will always be on your couch—but the most exciting seat is in the arena. In each of the chapters, there is a lesson learned—maybe they will help you reach your dream of being part of the action—maybe not playing in front of the crowd—but at least being part of the crowd and immersing yourself in the event at hand. I was never an "official" sports journalist or a connected team owner, so the stories that follow are examples of what many of us could do with a little effort and a bit of ingenuity and guile.

COTTON BOWL
1978

G rowing up as a Catholic in the 60s and 70s in the northern suburbs of Chicago, I was bombarded with Notre Dame press clippings and all around banter and propaganda–the Fighting Irish were "the" college football team virtually all boys followed and expected to win the National Championship.

   This hysteria was even more pronounced during high school, attending the largest Jesuit high school in the country–Loyola Academy. Although I decided not to enroll at Notre Dame, during my senior year in college, I was given an opportunity to attend the Cotton Bowl, pitting the Irish (ranked 3rd nationally before the game) against the No. 1 ranked team in the country–the Texas Longhorns. The game would be the equivalent of today's BCS Championship game.

Many of my friends went to Notre Dame and were planning to attend the game as they had access to tickets reserved for the respective student bodies. A week before the game, brokers were selling the tickets for close to $100, which does not sound expensive in today's dollars, but for 21-year-olds in the 70s that was a steep price. Fortunately, my Notre Dame friends were able to secure my cousin, Alan, and me two tickets, located in the end zone, naturally, but for the right price—$10 each (face value).

Interestingly, walking to the stadium on the day of the game there were many people (mainly scalpers) selling tickets—some for as low as $5. This experience would become a life lesson for my future attendance at sporting events—regardless of the so-called demand and popularity of an event, there are always tickets outside the stadium the day of the game. For whatever reason, people cannot go at the last minute to the most prestigious events—unplanned weddings, irreconcilable divorces, etc. Be patient, you'll get a ticket—someone else's misfortune will be your lucky opportunity.

When we arrived in Dallas for what essentially was the National Championship game, my cousin and I were greeted with 30 degree weather and recently fallen snow—obviously a rare occurrence for Texan weather at any time of the year. Little did we know that the weather would play a pivotal role in the outcome of the game, which would be the first major sporting event I would attend during my lifetime and serve as a motivating force to create a bucket list of sporting events to witness in person.

The game itself had little suspense, as Notre Dame won 38-10 in a convincing manner. The climax to the weekend was at the team's hotel when Notre Dame's head coach, Dan Devine, stood on the balcony of the hotel lobby and announced to the waiting Notre Dame fans that their team had just been crowned the No. 1 college team in the country. Pandemonium ensued, leading to a full night of celebration and otherwise rowdy behavior—that fortunately fell shy of jail time or a visit to the hospital (only an aching head for the train ride back home to Chicago.)

LESSON LEARNED:

Tap into your contacts, don't bite on the first offer, and don't let the "ticket demand" hype deter you from getting the ticket to a favorite event. Also, if you are at an age where prodigious amounts of beverages are consumed, you may want to cap your consumption so that your memory will recall these once-in-a-lifetime events.

Just remember, you're never too young (or too old) to witness a major sporting event—LIVE. I was 20 years old and took advantage of the ticket buying privileges my friends received from the college that they attended because their school had an excellent football team and went to Bowl games. However, if all of your friends attend Ivy League schools, it's very unlikely you'll be experiencing the BCS Bowl or any other in-demand Bowl game. Yet, those friends may become actual owners of a professional sports franchise, down the road, which could come in handy in your life.

MLB ALL-STAR GAME 1983

H aving watched baseball from the time I was nine years old on WGN-TV–the home of the Cubs and White Sox in the 60s and 70s, being able to attend a Major League Baseball All-Star Game–where baseball's greatest stars are showcased, was a dream come true.

In 1983, I was working for a Chicago radio station. For the six years I was at the station, I was very lucky to get to know the station's sports director, Red Mottlow, a legendary sports reporter in Chicago. Being a huge sports fan, I made it a point to talk with Red as often as possible and discuss the various Chicago teams during their respective seasons.

It was now the summer of 1983 and the All-Star Game was being held at historical Comiskey Park, home of the

White Sox, on the south side of Chicago. Badly wanting to go to the game, I told Red I would happily buy two tickets that he might come across. Well, a couple of weeks prior to the game, Red came into the station's sales office, where I worked, with the two tickets–great seats right behind home plate, about 25 rows from the field. Not only were the tickets great seats, they were for the right price–free.

I knew exactly who I would bring–my wife, Susan, of about 3 months. With both of us being long-standing Cubs fans, we cheered for the National League–an unfortunate choice for the night's event. The game was never in doubt, as the American League trounced the National League 13-3.

So, although the score was not the desired result, what a way to spend an evening–being with your new wife and watching one of baseball's greatest events, in your hometown. Not only were the tickets free, but since I was in radio, I convinced the parking attendant to let me into the press parking lot, where there was no admission fee. Oh, the beers were about $2 each, so I did have to air out my pockets a couple of times that night.

LESSON LEARNED:

If you happen to work in broadcasting or are part of the media, get to know the right people in your organization, who likely have access to hard-to-get tickets. Of course, if you are fortunate to receive any tickets from them, show your gratitude. I made a habit of sending plants to the Mottlow residence–I'm not sure Red appreciated them, but it always helps having the wife on your side.

And if you happen to be recently married, presuming your spouse is a sports fan, it's usually a good idea to invite her/him, rather than a neighbor, college roommate, or business colleague–the invitation is a positive step in solidifying your matrimonial commitment.

SUPER BOWL
1986

The 1985 Bears team was one of the most heralded football team in history. In 2012 *Sports Illustrated* ranked them as the greatest single season NFL team of all time—in any era. They lost only one game during the season and dominated with an invincible defense and an offense headed by Jim McMahon, the "punky" QB, and Walter Payton, considered by many as the greatest player (but not necessarily greatest runner) of all time.

In November of the 1985 season, sensing this could be the year for the Bears to make their first Super Bowl appearance, I began to make arrangements to see them play in this most-watched sporting event in America. I first made my flight reservation, which was to Biloxi, Mississippi, because the few flights into New Orleans, the venue for the game, were sold out. Secondly, I contacted my cousin, Alan, who was living in New Orleans with his wife, Mamie, to see if they would allow my wife, Susan, and me to stay with them. Since Alan and I have been close for over 35 years, he was happy to have us.

But now, thirdly, was really the hard part–securing tickets to the game. In 1985, I was employed by a national broadcasting company and put in my request for four tickets. Now the only remaining issue was for the Bears to make it to the game. They eventually finished the season 13-1 and in the two playoff games, shutout their opponents–the New York Giants and Los Angeles Rams. They were going to the Super Bowl!

The question was whether I would be going to the Super Bowl and lucky enough to get the tickets I had previously requested eight weeks ago from my employer. The day after the Bears finished winning their second playoff game, my boss informed me that I would receive four tickets to the game–supposedly the only person at my company to receive four for their personal use! Not only was I the only person to receive four tickets–they were complimentary ($75 face)–the stars were lined up for sure. The Bears would be going to the Super Bowl in New Orleans, playing the New England Patriots–and I would be there to witness this once-in-a-lifetime event!

We arrived in Biloxi that Friday and were picked up at the airport by Alan. That night, after a quick homemade meal, we began to indulge in the beginning of the Super Bowl experience. We headed down to the French Quarter where Bears fans, and some Patriot fans, were fully participating in full pre-Super Bowl celebrations. After having sampled a number of New Orleans' finest beverages, we tested our constitution–in a very unique way.

Alan, who managed the tallest building in New Orleans at the time, the Shell Building, brought the four of us to the top of the building—the actual roof itself, 50 stories above the ground level creatures and vehicles. Here we were, each having consumed a number of mind-altering beverages, prancing around the rooftop of the city's tallest building that, by the way, had no railing just in case you lost your balance—trying to get a better view of the cars and pedestrians 50 stories below us.

OK, well we survived that adventure to have a more tranquil Saturday, making sure we were in good shape for the main event. That Sunday, we lounged around the house watching a few of the pre-game shows, before embarking downtown to the game itself.

As much of a thrill as it was to see the game, it was rather un-suspenseful—the Bears easily won 46-10, the biggest landslide in Super Bowl history at that time. The Bears managed to score in every conceivable way, with the exception of having Walter Payton score, a slight disappointment. Outside of the Bears' dominating play, the other highlight was during halftime, when the *Super Bowl Shuffle*, a music video which many of the Bears recorded in November (ironically after their only loss of the season to the Miami Dolphins) was played throughout the stadium— the crowd went berserk and it was a prelude to the team winning the Super Bowl and the four of us returning to the French Quarter to conclude a wild weekend. Leaving the following day for Chicago was a necessary recovery period, but one filled with a lifetime of sensational memories!

LESSON LEARNED:

Have faith in your team and make a commitment to see them perform on the national stage—even when their appearance is uncertain, which may be months before the big event, itself. It also helps to have relatives in the city where the event takes place and be employed by a company that has access to such tickets. And, by all means, don't be afraid to ask for those cherished tickets—promise your boss that your efforts at contributing to the company's success will be commensurate with the company's efforts to help you attend the event in question—that should be good fodder for the water cooler. Oh, and it is critical to have your prayers answered (usually out of your control), allowing your team to end on a successful note—participating in the big show and being crowned the World Champions.

WORLD SERIES
1987

Knowing that my chances of attending a World Series involving my favorite team at the time, the Chicago Cubs, were almost as good as owning the team itself, I decided to attend the next best thing–attend a World Series in St. Louis, watching the Cardinals (the Cubs' archrival) play the Minnesota Twins. On business, I was in St. Louis for the fourth game of the Series (second in St. Louis), staying at the Marriott Hotel, located right across the street from Busch Stadium, the venue for the game.

Once again, I needed to find a ticket. Little did I know, I would end up with something better than a ticket–I was able to secure a Press Pass as a result of a little creative storytelling.

Having left broadcasting and the company where I

worked the previous year, I still had my old ID card, which I was never asked to return upon my departure from the company. The media credentials area was in my hotel–convenient for me. I entered the media room and requested my press credentials for the game. Hmmmm, the person distributing the credentials couldn't find mine–what a surprise. I responded that I was filling in for the sports director of a local Chicago television station, (whose name I conveniently could not remember) as a result of food poisoning that the sports director had contracted.

At this point, I was instructed to go across the street to Busch Stadium and talk to Mr. O'Connor from Major League Baseball. After telling my story of filling in for a sick sports director, Mr. O'Connor gave me a Press Pass, which allowed me access to the field and press box. But, he said, the pass did not give me access to the clubhouse and wanted to make sure I was OK with that–"Well, I guess that will work, Mr. O'Connor," I said, pinching myself to keep from laughing.

I was in the stadium at 5:30 for the 7 pm game and spent the next hour on the field during batting practice, snagging a couple of balls for mementos and acting like I was about to interview Whitey Herzog, the Cardinals manager, in his dugout–oops, not enough time, so I better get up to the press box to begin reporting on the night's game and preparing to "file my story."

Once I was in the press box and sat down, I had a phone in front of me, which I promptly used to call friends and business associates in Chicago–long distance, of course, on Major League Baseball's dime (better than calling collect in those days). One person who I called, specifically, was a friend and former business colleague, still employed in broadcasting, a huge Cardinals fan and watching the game on television (maybe from his couch). I, on the other hand, had "retired" from broadcasting, was viewing the game from the press box, at the World Series, no less, and had no interest in either team. Irony?

Since I was neither a Cardinals or Twins fan, the details of the game became virtually irrelevant to me—although I do know the Cardinals emerged victorious. I returned to the Marriott that night, overjoyed that I had just watched my first World Series game from the press box, after being on the field and retrieving a World Series ball, no less. And I still had access to the next game, the following day. However, I would be leaving St. Louis the next morning and would forfeit the opportunity to see another World Series game during the 1987 Series—which eventually was won by the Minnesota Twins.

LESSON LEARNED:

Take full advantage of your storytelling talents and be nice and respectful to those who may feel sorry for your pathetic desperation to make it to a World Series game. And be prepared to tell your story to more than one person (remember how you would talk to your father, if your mother didn't give you what you wanted—apply the same philosophy in these situations), because not everyone will buy your story. But, hey, all you need is one person to believe you, and you're set—exhaust all possible personnel options! And once you have an entrée onto the field or press box, try to control your star struck amazement and act as if you are behind in filing your story—like a real reporter.

NBA ALL-STAR
GAME
1988

Michael Jordan had been playing basketball for the Chicago Bulls for four years when the NBA All-Star game was being played in his new, adopted hometown–Chicago. I was fortunate to have watched Jordan play those early years in Chicago, but, now, here was another opportunity to watch basketball's greatest stars–Larry Bird, Magic Johnson and Michael Jordan play in front of a home crowd.

I very much wanted to witness this special game of showmanship in Chicago, but the demand for a ticket was outrageous. Ticket brokers were getting astronomical premiums–5-10 times face value, depending on the seat location. Since I did not have that type of discretionary income, I was left with trying to buy a ticket from a scalper or a friend, one of whom might have tickets and were willing to invite me to the game with them.

Well, no friend came to my aid, so that Saturday–Showtime day–I left for the game, with no ticket, about three hours before tipoff, hoping that some soul would need to get rid of his ticket. Well, my luck struck about an hour before game time and I paid slightly more than the $50 face value. The price was right; however, there was only one small issue–my ticket had an obstructed view behind a pillar. Since I was not willing to endure viewing any action obstructed during this star-studded event, I had to figure a way to maximize my live-viewing potential.

Once again, my plan was to replicate history and copy my World Series strategy, by sitting in the press box. At least I had a ticket and was in the legendary Chicago Stadium–now I just had to maneuver my way to the press box that overlooked the far end of the court. That day I was wearing a navy blue sport coat (attire that would come in handy over the years), making me look somewhat responsible and conceivably even important (maybe not such an apt description of the media).

So, I climbed up to the press box and there was an usher tending to the needs of one of the local Chicago sportswriters–a legitimate member of the media. Fortunately, the usher did not have to attend to any of my needs and so, as he was preoccupied with an honestly credentialed member of the press, I made my way into the relatively crowded press box area, promptly sat down in the only available open chair, and wrote my name on the place card in front of me on the counter top where the real scribes were reporting the details and highlights of the game–JEFFREY JACOBS (virtually all of the press would not need to have their name placed in front of them–because they were known–I was not.)

At this point, my view of the game was perfectly clear–no

people in front of me and no over-hanging or misplaced steel beam to obstruct my view of the game and its superstars. All I needed to do was get myself one of the beverages, generously provided by Chicago Stadium, sit back and keep my fingers crossed that I would be accepted into this media fraternity.

Oh, yes, the game. It was great; Jordan scored 40 points and was named the game's MVP. The East beat the West 138-133 and my day at Chicago Stadium, attending the first NBA All-Star game in Chicago's history, was a complete success!

LESSON LEARNED:

Never get discouraged that your contacts or connections have not helped you secure the ticket that you want and need. Be patient, get in the door for a minimal price, look for the opportunity to "be upgraded," be bold, look like you belong and blend in—you won't regret it!

THE CHICAGO
CUBS' FIRST
NIGHT GAME
8/8/88

Clearly, a typical August night baseball game would not rank as a major sporting event. However, in this instance, an exception needs to be made. Of all Chicago sports teams, the Cubs were the team I had followed the longest, since the mid 60s, when I was eight years old and they were only about 50 percent of the way into their drought of not winning a World Series. I religiously watched their games on WGN and attended Cubs games many times over the years in their landmark Wrigley Field. At this time in 1988, they obviously had established quite a record for both futility and tradition–having only played games in the daylight. Finally, the team was ready to break tradition–but still retained its commitment to futility.

On a numerically memorable date, 8/8/88, the Cubs

played their first night game—ever! Given that this was a milestone in both their history and for the game of baseball, tickets, once again, were exorbitantly expensive and virtually impossible to get. But as we have heard so often, "It's not what you know, it's who you know." In this instance, fortunately for me, I had a friend, Jim George, who worked at WGN radio and was allotted four tickets to this exceptional nighttime event. Given that I had gently reminded him, incessantly, for months after the date was announced of my interest in attending the game, he succumbed to my constant pressure—"UNCLE!"—and invited me to join him, his wife and daughter.

Being the gracious guest, I treated them to a delectable Mexican dinner prior to the game—a whopping $40 value, for a ticket valued at hundreds of dollars (thank you, Jim!) Thirty minutes before game-time, we entered the majestic field, illuminated for the first time. The crowd was awestruck by the beauty and significance of the experience. And when I mention crowd, I'm talking about the hordes of national celebrities, who had to be there—Bill Murray, George Will, the mayor, etc. This was a happening that would not repeat itself—akin to the Cubs making a World Series appearance. As a matter of fact, when a team does not succeed in winning their sport's respective championship, the motto is "Wait until next year." In the Cubs' case, it was "Wait until next century"—which happened 28 years later—FINALLY.

So, the four of us took our seats and watched all of the obligatory ceremonies, with various Cubs stars and dignitaries speaking to commemorate the event. When the game finally started, which, by the way, included the Philadelphia Phillies, as the Cubs opponent, dark clouds rapidly approached. By the 4th inning, the rain was coming down with considerable force and, eventually, caused the game to be rained out, with the Cubs leading 3-1. After all the hype, planning, ceremonies, etc., their "first" night game was actually an exercise in futility—typical for the Cubs and typical, also, for Cubs fans. The official first night game was played the following day and the final score, after a legitimate nine inning game, was Cubs 6, Phillies 4.

LESSON LEARNED:

Pick your friends wisely and always remind them of how important your friendship is—especially spending precious moments with them at rare sporting events where they plan to attend with their personal tickets and may have an extra one for you. And, certainly, while you're the guest at this special game, look for ways to repay their generosity—chip in for a couple of beers, a box of Cracker Jack, maybe some cotton candy—even a hearty, sit-down Mexican meal, if you're really in a giving mood.

In 1989, the PGA Championship was played at Kemper Lakes, a public course located in Riverwoods, Illinois–a northwest Chicago suburb. This would be my first major golf tournament attendance as a spectator, and it meant a bit more to me because I had played Kemper several times since it had opened, a few years earlier. No doubt, I was acutely aware of my golf game's limitations, prior to attending this tournament. But when you see the pros hit shots on the same holes you have played many times, you get a totally new sense of appreciation for their skill and your, or my, lack of it. It is quite exciting to see their prodigious drives, precise iron shots and adroit putts–all very humbling to a hacker like myself.

At the time, I worked for an investment management

firm, who had a tent during the tournament for client entertainment. It was wonderful to experience an event like this in such grandeur–legitimately. Attending the final day, it was terrific witnessing the crowning of a major tournament champion–in this instance, Payne Stewart. There was no chicanery or suspense in my attendance, but the 1989 PGA Championship whetted my taste for future golf majors that will be represented later in this book.

LESSON LEARNED:

If it pays to know the right people, it also is beneficial to work for the right company, who believes in entertaining their clients at major sporting events. Always volunteer for these opportunities. And, if you volunteer frequently, who knows, not only will your ticket stub collection grow, but possibly, you'll be rewarded with a larger pay stub at bonus time–double your pleasure.

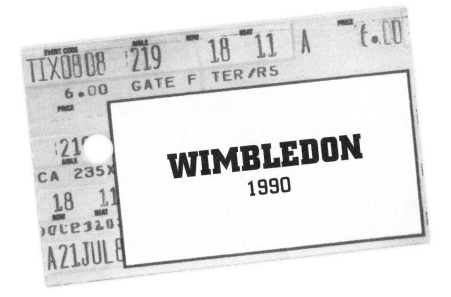

WIMBLEDON
1990

In 1990, my wife and I made travel plans to visit England—mainly the areas outside of London, such as the Cotswolds and other idyllic towns in the countryside. We would visit in early July, just as the Wimbledon tournament was in its second week. Since I had been a tennis fan and player for over 25 years, attending a world famous Wimbledon tennis match was something that we had to include in our England itinerary.

As we planned our trip, it looked like we would be staying outside of London during the semi-finals matches—where ticket demand was enormously high. You see, Wimbledon attracts not just a British crowd, but people all throughout Europe, and other continents—it truly is a global event—with universal demand for tickets. By the spring of that year, still several months before the matches were to be played, I went to work on securing tickets.

First, my father's very good friend was the past President of NBC Sports. Since the tournament is broadcast by NBC, I thought he might be able to help out. Well, either he didn't have the pull he once had with his past employees at NBC or I didn't have the pull with him—because that avenue did not produce any tickets.

The second approach was to contact my current employer's London office to see if they might have any connections for Wimbledon. After several weeks of anxiously waiting, the answer came back—NO, sorry, we can't help you (I assume the answer may have been different if my position within the company was a bit loftier than a third-year institutional sales person).

The third option was to contact a ticket broker—they are usually the last and most expensive option. And in this case, history repeated itself—tickets for the semi-finals were selling for $750 each—about what our lodging was going to cost for our entire 10 day England trip. I let the broker sell his Wimbledon tickets to another bloke—one more desperate than me, one, maybe, wealthier than me, or one, maybe, just more moronic than me.

Although we did not have a Wimbledon ticket before leaving for England, I knew we would attempt to see a match at the hallowed tennis shrine once we were in the near vicinity. On a Saturday, we arrived in the town of Wimbledon and walked over to the universally known tennis complex. A little luck would happen, as we were able to buy two tickets to the women's doubles semi-finals matches on Court 1, adjacent to Centre Court, where the men's semi-finals singles matches were being played. If you queued up at the ticket window, you could buy tickets from patrons who were leaving the tournament.

Now that we were on the grounds within the Wimbledon

tennis area, I tried to convince the Wimbledon media relations group, once again producing my former broadcasting company's ID card, to give my wife and me access to the men's semi-finals matches. The best they could do was to give me, alone, access to such privileges. In order to both preserve the remaining part of the trip's itinerary, along with my marriage, I thanked them for their offer, and graciously declined. This is one reason why attending events, solo, is so much more successful.

During the women's doubles matches, featuring Garrison/Fendick (US) vs Novotny/Sukova (Czech), I decided to take a "bathroom" break. This break consisted of going to Centre Court, conveniently adjacent to Court 1 where I had my ticket, and schmoozing the security guard who was protecting the photographer's pit, actually on the court itself, with my "charming" Chicaaago accent. After I produced my handy, always available, and outdated ID card, and a camera that was a shade more sophisticated than a Polaroid, the guard escorted me to the photographer's pit on Centre Court—here I am at Wimbledon's Centre Court in the photographer's pit, where their equipment/lenses are longer than my arm. I'm watching Ivan Lendl and Stefan Edberg, with Lady Di and Fergie in the Royal Box. This is nirvana—except that I'm solo and my wife is now thinking I have a bad case of dysentery or am pulling another stunt—for which she will be likely putting me in another type of box, absent any Royal treatment.

Well, I took pictures with my remedial snapshot camera for over 30 minutes, waved to the lovely ladies in the Royal Box (without receiving an acknowledgement), and finally made my way back to Court 1 to watch the final minutes of that match (which became so insignificant, I cannot remember who actually won.) As I returned, I was greeted by a rather skeptical wife, who by this time was getting all too accustomed to my squirrelly adventures and had absolutely no interest in hearing about my latest escapade–regardless of who was or was not waving to me.

LESSON LEARNED:

Plan ahead, although this did not produce success; in this case, be persistent and take any ticket you can get to any match (be sure to queue up), be married to an understanding wife (or husband, for those female sports fanatics) and use any charm you think you have to improve your "status" at the event. Also, when you return to be with your wife/husband, after your "brief" separation, flatter her/him by exclaiming she is more beautiful/he is more handsome than any Royal family member–it will help diminish the rudeness of your absence.

The NCAA Final Four basketball tournament, by the mid 1980's, had become one of the hottest tickets in sports. Because of its popularity, the venues were moved to larger stadiums whose capacity could accommodate 50,000 plus people. I was not a huge college basketball fan and still rarely even participate in the ubiquitous pools that dominate March Madness. However, attending the Final Four was an event that promised excitement, suspense, skill and relative purity in a sports world that was becoming dominated by money.

In 1991, I was still an institutional salesperson at an investment management firm and had clients all throughout the Midwest. The Final Four that year was played in Indianapolis, where I had two good clients. Since tickets to the Final Four were, essentially, sold as a package of both the semi-finals and finals games, I was not willing to spend the time (Saturday and Monday, when the three games were played) and the money to see all three games–especially, since none of my favorite teams were playing.

However, I did plan a business trip to have lunch with a client that Monday afternoon of the actual Finals, conveniently allowing me to attend the Championship game, if I were able to procure a ticket. After lunch, I drove to the RCA Dome, where the Championship game would be played to see if there were any tickets being sold by anyone–are you kidding, there were hundreds available!

Here's the lowdown: after the semi-finals games are completed, the fans of the two losing teams, typically, have tickets to the Finals, too, but usually have no interest in sticking around to see two other teams battle for the title, after their team has just lost. So, after their respective semi-finals game, they sell their tickets to scalpers, who try to re-sell the tickets that Sunday and Monday, which does not allow much time to sell the huge supply of tickets. Hence, there is an abundance of tickets that are very reasonably priced.

The Championship Final was between Duke and Kansas–two marquee names. I actually bought a ticket that afternoon for $75–$25 over face, and located nine rows in back of the basket, from a UNLV fan. Essentially, the ticket to the Finals, itself, is one of the easiest tickets to get in sports. Now, if you need to go to the semi-finals, that's another story and one where I can offer no advice.

The game was fairly unmemorable, with the exception that Duke won, (85-80), recording their first NCAA Basketball Championship. From my perspective, as a fan of neither Duke or Kansas, the game was not terribly rowdy, since only about half the stadium was passionate for one of the teams–the event caters to a huge corporate crowd of sponsors and clients, who are relatively indifferent to what's occurring on the court. However, they are not so indifferent to the heavy array of beverages that are available off the court. As such, although I am glad I knocked this game off my bucket list, it's too bad, from my perspective, the energy of the crowd was significantly lower than most sporting events I have attended, including regular season contests, where no title is at stake.

LESSON LEARNED:

If you are not choosy about seeing only the Finals, without the semi-finals, plan a trip to the city hosting the tournament that Monday and sharpen your negotiation skills with the army of scalpers, holding hundreds of tickets—who must unload them in a matter of hours. You'll be surprised at the ease of buying a ticket—the bigger challenge is getting transportation to the venue city and finding accommodations. Hopefully, your favorite team will be in the finals, because if they are not, and you are there for just the experience, it could be a rather hum drum affair.

Although baseball was the first sport I watched, hockey was my favorite in the 60s and 70s. During that period, the Chicago Blackhawks were Chicago's most competitive team and tickets to the games were the most difficult to secure. Crowds at Chicago Stadium, where the Blackhawks played, were consistently sold out and the loudest in hockey—according to virtually all of the broadcasters and players of the opposing teams.

So, now the NHL All-Star game is going to be played in the loudest stadium in hockey—my favorite sport to watch, especially in person. However, again, I had no legitimate access to a good ticket. But, on this day, I drove to the Stadium, parked my car (in the expected media lot) and was approached by a scalper. I bought the nosebleed seat for $40 and made my way into the stadium.

Again, if you have any hope of maneuvering at a sporting event, you must have the appearance of looking somewhat important—what better way to achieve that look than to wear the uniformly accepted blue blazer—my favorite, which I did. After entering the stadium about an hour before the opening face-off, I explored different places where I might watch this battle, outside of the seat listed on my ticket. Hey, how about the press box again—free food and drink, plenty of seat space, unobstructed views and no worries about some inebriated or just clumsy fan spilling their beer on you.

OK, now that I had my destination goal decided, all I had to do was make it happen. The press box at Chicago Stadium, as you may remember from an earlier chapter, was at the end of the rink, above the mezzanine seats. After climbing the stairs to the box, I encountered the expected security usher, who was more interested in acknowledging and chatting with his familiar media friends than checking my credentials. As he was engaged in another conversation with a local sports writer, I promptly put my head down and strolled confidently, yet, casually, toward "my seat." While the usher was engaged with his friend, I was engaged with my seat.

After acclimating to the press scene and making sure I would be here for the duration of the game, I decided to help myself to the beautiful spread the NHL and Blackhawk organization made available to the international, national, and local media, who would be reporting on this annual hockey classic that had not been played in Chicago for many years. Little did the hosts know that I, too, would enjoy their hospitality, but without any reporting.

The day was going quite well: I parked my car in the media parking lot for no charge, bought a scalped ticket for face value, made my way to the press box and helped myself to all the food and beverages I wanted. I was now prepared to watch the game—the reason for my attendance.

The interesting thing about this game is that it was played three days after the 1991 Gulf War (Operation Desert Storm) started—a rather nervous time for America and our troops, as we were in conflict with a, supposedly, highly trained and effective Red Unit of the Iraqi army. During this period, patriotism was at an all-time high—far greater than during the Vietnam War, fought 20 years earlier. Given the coincidental timing of the game and Mideast war, emotions for the game were the highest I have ever experienced during any sporting event—ever! Essentially, the game was virtually overshadowed by the bigger event overseas.

Before the game started, the obligatory *National Anthem* was sung by, legendary, Wayne Messmer. Chicago Stadium was renowned for the noise the crowd created during the typical National Anthem, let alone one that was to be played during such an emotional time period like this war. As the Anthem was playing, the stadium reverberated, resembling a national pep rally—banners, flags, lighters, etc. were proudly waved throughout the air. You could barely see the faces in the crowd and the decibel level was off the charts—Pat Foley, the Blackhawks announcer, later described the scene as sounding like the Concord taking off—an accurate description.

At the conclusion of this rousing Anthem, Pat Foley asked for a few moments of silence to recognize our boys in Kuwait. You now have 20,000 out of control fans, who, for several minutes, sang the *Star Spangled Banner* at the top of their lungs silenced—very briefly. This was truly a surreal moment in sports, until one lone voice echoed throughout the stadium "Kick Saddam's Ass"—prompting the 20,000 people to unravel into total bedlam in the stands—all before the puck had even dropped.

This spectacular outpouring of emotions was replayed later that afternoon on CNN. Coincidentally, General Schwartzkopf, who was leading our country's war efforts in the Mideast, saw a clip of this momentous *National Anthem* and was so moved by it that he requested 5,000 copies to be distributed to the troops–so they could "feel" the support back home. The following day in the paper, Wayne Gretzky, hockey's greatest player, ever, was quoted as saying that "there couldn't have been a dry eye" in the place–it was one unbelievably emotional five minutes.

Oh, by the way, the game almost became an afterthought. The West beat the East 12-7, in another show of offensiveness that has become normal in these types of contests.

LESSON LEARNED:

Repeat successes experienced at previously attended events–wear an "official" looking outfit, get a reasonably priced ticket into the venue, assess various seating opportunities and finally resort to becoming a member of the press, once again–looking and acting like you belong.

An interesting footnote to my experience in the press box this day was witnessing Chicago's legendary (and late) ABC broadcaster, Tim Weigel, arriving a bit late for the game and, as a result, did not have his "reserved" seat, which had already been taken (by you know who). Tim ended up standing for the game–you've heard the saying "You snooze, you lose."

Just remember, since the press sits most of the day writing their stories, they may actually appreciate the diversion of standing for the duration of a 3 hour game. We all know that standing keeps us more alert–possibly, their standing and your sitting will make their writing even crisper and more entertaining than usual–you're doing the press a good service–good for you!

I n 1991, the Chicago Bulls, with the legendary Michael Jordan, made it to their first NBA Finals and would play the Los Angeles Lakers. This was a marquee match-up, pitting Jordan against Magic Johnson–a battle for the ages.

During the 1991 series, the Bulls lost the first game, but proceeded to win the next three in a row. I then decided I would attend the fifth game, which would be played in LA and, potentially, end up being the game that the Bulls clinched to become the NBA Champions–another once-in-a-lifetime opportunity. Immediately after they won their third game, I made my flight reservation to LA, which would be played three nights later–Wednesday, June 12th. Getting an airline ticket was no problem and quite affordable, using my frequent flyer miles. My flight would arrive that Wednesday afternoon and I would then take the red-eye back to Chicago, land at 5 am to catch a 7 am flight to St. Louis for client meetings that were scheduled.

That Sunday night, after they won their third game, I called my boss about my plan—he was all for it. Once more, I had my transportation to the game, would not need accommodations, but would, of course, have to find a ticket. Brokers were selling tickets to game five in LA for several hundreds of dollars—easily five times face value. The only reason ticket prices were not higher is because LA fans may have felt they would see the Lakers lose and the Bulls win the Championship—not so great for them. And Chicago fans likely did not want to take the time and effort to visit LA for a game that might not end with the Bulls winning. I was willing to take that chance.

So, my plan was to take advantage of the fickle LA fans and figure that there would be plenty of tickets around the LA Forum, the game's venue, that Wednesday afternoon, several hours before tip-off. Fortunately, I was right. I managed to buy a ticket from a local, trustworthy scalper (sometimes an oxymoronic term) for $100 (compared to $40 face)—a steal given the magnitude of the game from a Chicago Bulls fan's perspective and, potentially, seeing them win their inaugural NBA Championship.

Given the fashionably late arriving LA crowd, I watched the first half of the game about 10 rows from the court by the free throw line—an even better value for my $100 than where my assigned seat was located. My luck lasted only so long and the actual ticketholder finally arrived for the second half, requiring me to view most of the final half from my second level ticket location.

At this time, it didn't matter where I was sitting. I wanted to witness sports history for a Chicago team. The Bulls were losing halfway through the fourth quarter, when John Paxson, their reliable, but not flashy, guard began hitting basket after basket—including some three pointers, to put the Bulls in the lead. With about two minutes remaining, it became apparent the Bulls would win the game. LA fans, true to their fickle nature, began streaming out of the Forum, allowing me to watch the last couple of minutes from about five rows off the floor, by the Bulls bench, standing next to Darryl Hannah, a well-known Hollywood star, who looked like your average librarian—really (and she probably thought I looked like your average book worm).

Once the game concluded with the Bulls winning 108-101, I ran onto the court, which became quite a mob scene, with hundreds of Bulls fans in attendance. Elbows were flying, mixed in with high-fives—the court resembled a mosh pit and I was fortunate to get out of there with no medical attention required—or my face moshed in.

I caught a cab from The Forum to LA International for my 11:30 red-eye flight back to Chicago. The flight left on time, landed on time, and I was now on my way to St. Louis for a full day's worth of client meetings. There I recounted my latest sports caper to various St. Louis financial executives, who became more tired listening to my tales than I was fatigued from the previous 24-hour activity marathon. I guess when "they asked for the time," I told them "how to make the watch, too."

It was a great way to play hooky and cost me essentially the $100 ticket, $50 cab fares, allowing for a few beers and snacks at the game. I now had seen two Chicago teams win their respective championships!

LESSON LEARNED:

If your team wins their third game, in their respective sport's championship series, (presuming it's a best out of seven series) make plans, immediately, to see them win the potential championship game—especially if the game is out of town. In these instances, hometown fans are more reluctant to go to the game and, possibly, see their team eliminated. Hence, there are two benefits—tickets are easier to get and they are cheaper than if their team was on the cusp of winning the championship, rather than losing the final game.

Also, make the flight arrangements, perhaps using frequent flyer miles, and start contacting people you may know in the visiting team's city where the game is played. And if no leads materialize, resort to utilizing the predictable horde of ticket scalpers that will surround the game's venue. Take your time, don't be desperate, and you'll likely get your desired ticket for a small premium over face value.

The he largest paid audience for a one-day sporting event
in the world is the Indianapolis 500—with over 400,000
spectators viewing the race LIVE (some in a sober state)
from the Indianapolis Motor Speedway. The track is so
big there are four holes of an 18 hole golf course in the
Speedway's infield.

To say I was or am a huge car race fan would be a gross
overstatement. Although in my teens, I owned a couple
of GTO's (the era's hotrods)—one of which had the brakes
go out as I was coming home from college. On that given
day, I was in a hurry to get home and traveling a bit over
the speed limit—110 mph to be exact. And in this specific
stretch home from DePauw University, located in the
midst of some of the nation's most scintillating cornfields,

there was not a highway in sight—only rural roads, just to make things more exciting. You get the picture: 19-year-old college student driving home from a little known campus on a rural road—at 110 mph, slowing down to make a turn onto another rural road. Oops, brakes not working, the brake pedal is, actually, now on the floorboard, and I'm trying to make a turn at, well, just under Mach I, or so it seemed. Grab your helmets everybody. Fortunately, the gods were with me—I avoided a collision and made my way home safely and will now continue with my Indy story.

The Indy 500 was one of those sporting spectaculars that should be experienced at least once in your life. At the time, I had clients in Indy who had access to a couple of tickets for the race. I gladly paid face value for the tickets—$45—and invited a high school friend, Mike Garofalo, to join me.

Well, it just so happened that Mike was a pilot and, coincidentally, he had a client who wanted Mike to fly him (and two of his friends) to the Indy 500 on the client's plane. Perfect. I had the tickets; Mike had the transportation—a private plane (a nice trade off). So we all (5 of us in total) left from Palwaukee Airport, located in Palatine, outside of Chicago, for Indianapolis that Memorial Day morning. We landed safely and made arrangements to meet back at the plane, (since the owner and his friends had seats on the other side of the track from ours) sharply at 3:30, giving us what we thought would be plenty of time to see the race from start to finish.

On this Memorial Day, the weather was in the 30's, with a wind chill of less than 32 degrees, very unseasonably chilly for Indy at that time of the year. Because of the cold, the cars could not grip the track very well at their 200 mph speeds and, consequently, there were more crashes than at a driving school serving spiked beverages.

Because of these cold conditions, the race went on forever—when there is a crash, all cars have to reduce their speed, and stay in the same position as they were before the crash occurred, until the accident has been removed. From a spectator's perspective, the so-called excitement of the crashes was balanced by the low average 130 mph speeds—the slowest for the Indy 500 at that time in nearly 35 years. One of the highlights was walking underneath the track to get a warm beverage, and listening to the roaring cars racing above us—it sounded like we were in the middle of a war zone. Unfortunately, since so much time of the race was spent in formation, waiting for another accident to be cleared, there would have been more excitement watching bowling on the local cable station.

By 3:15, 15 minutes before we were supposed to meet the owner of the plane, only about 75% of the race was completed. We could not leave now since the race was far from over. At 4 pm, the race was still running, but Mike felt we better get back to the plane in case the owner's patience for such a slow Indy 500 had been exhausted. Not only was his patience exhausted, he was beside himself waiting for Mike, the pilot, and me—the freeloader. As we approached the plane, we could see a stream of smoke forming from the owner's ears—it looked similar to the aftermath of many of the crashes on the track that afternoon.

It was pretty funny seeing this wealthy guy having to wait for the pilot (and his lackey buddy) for over half an hour—he was on time and we were not. The flight home was chillier than the race itself—too bad; how could the guy leave this momentous, albeit s-l-o-w, race early?!

The double whammy here is that, not only were we late to the plane, compromising Mike's client relationship, we also missed the last lap of the race, which was won by Al Unser by less than one second—the closest race in the history of the Indianapolis 500. We missed the final lap by about a minute and were late to arrive to the plane by more than 30 minutes. Life is all about timing, right?

LESSON LEARNED:

In this case, my contacts came through for tickets and I had one of my best friends provide first class transportation–a rare luxury for me. The biggest lesson was committing two mistakes at the race–not seeing the race's historically close finish (the closest ever) and causing a client relationship to almost disintegrate (like some of the unfortunate race cars). Next time, I'll know better to honor a time commitment or experience the finale of the attending event.

Baseball, football, basketball, hockey, tennis and golf are all sports I have played at one time or another in my life. Conspicuous by its absence is soccer–I never played the sport (and some might say I didn't play a number of the aforementioned ones, too), although I have tremendous respect for those who do or did. And as has been documented for years, soccer is the world's, not America's, favorite sport and the World Cup is the tournament where the best soccer teams represent their respective countries by competing against each other every four years. As such, the World Cup Final is viewed by more people, internationally, than any other one-day sporting event.

In 1994, for the first time in its history, the World Cup games were played in the US at various cities. The

Opening game and Opening Ceremonies, on the same day, occurred in Chicago and the Final in Los Angeles, all of which I wanted to attend and was fortunate to do so.

At the time, my wife was the Director of the Illinois Department of Tourism Department. One of her colleagues served on a committee that interfaced with the World Cup organization, FIFA, and was able to get tickets for both the Opening and Final game. The Opening Ceremonies and first World Cup game were showcased in Chicago's legendary Soldier Field, and featured Bolivia and Germany, the World Cup defending champion. The Opening Ceremony festivities were sensational–President Clinton spoke and the renowned diva, Diana Ross, sang the National Anthem. My wife and I sat behind one of the goals in the first row on a sweltering day, filled with lots of excitement and spectators from all over the world. It was a fantastic day because of the game's significance–the first time a World Cup game was played on US soil. The game's final score, Germany 1, Bolivia 0, was somewhat incidental.

Several weeks later, I would experience the World Cup Final in LA, featuring Italy against Brazil. The game would be viewed on television by over a billion people. My brother, Chris, joined me for the game, where we arrived a couple of hours beforehand in the famous Rose Bowl in Pasadena. Little did I know, as we entered the grounds outside the stadium, I would encounter three unique individuals that afternoon.

Strolling the Rose Bowl grounds, I noticed a recent celebrity on his way into the stadium–Robert Shapiro, who was ubiquitous at that time, representing OJ Simpson, now better known for his actions off the field than on it. I pointed him out to my brother, who instantly gave me his camera and had me take a picture of the two of them together. Chris may have figured that knowing Mr. Shapiro could come in handy one day–so far it hasn't (and hopefully, it won't).

The temperatures that day hovered around 100 degrees and people outside were passing out all over, keeping the paramedics busy. If this were a concert, there may have been other factors besides the heat causing spectator collapse, but today, only Mother Nature was the cause.

With about an hour before the game, I decided to enter the Stadium myself—Chris would continue to look for celebrities on the grounds. My goal, entering the Rose Bowl so early, was solely to meet Pelé—soccer's most legendary star. Given the nearly 100,000 fans attending the game, meeting Pelé, who would be broadcasting for one of the international networks, was a bit of a pipe dream.

Once inside the Rose Bowl, I headed for the media section, which consisted of about 40 rows in the middle of one side of the stadium—essentially between the 40-yard lines. At the end of each row stood security guards, wearing purple berets, checking the credentials of the international press, who were here to report back to the 100+ countries that would follow the contest. Of course, I was not a member of the world- wide press, and naturally, did not have the credentials to show the security guards—what else is new.

Well, once again, adopting my favorite philosophy, "Act like you belong," I casually strolled up the steps trying to figure out which guard looked the most bored, dis-interested in his job, and least motivated to ask me for my credentials. At about the 20th row, I found one of the purple beret wearing guards engaged in conversation with a foreign speaking media member. As he was focused on this individual, likely trying to understand the reporter's language, I nonchalantly walked into the row—"confirming" that my ticket was located in the area where I was now standing.

Walking down the row, I decided to approach the mid-point—about the 50-yard line—where my vantage was just perfect. For the next 45 minutes, I was standing with the press from the Swiss and Czech media teams. Although I did not understand any of their pre-game commentary, I did understand how very fortunate I was to be amongst the most celebrated sports media at the most watched sporting event in the world—with the best seat in the house. Talk about fantasy; how could it get any better? Well, it would.

Shockingly, who would walk down the row just in front of mine and promptly take his seat directly in front of me—yes, Pelé, himself! Indeed, the planets were lined up! Of all the rows and seats I could have selected in this huge stadium, somehow, I managed to select the one spot just behind where Pelé would be broadcasting. After composing myself, I politely asked Pelé to sign my ticket stub, offering him my pen. Graciously, he used his own pen and signed my ticket with a broad smile—I was out of my mind!

My next decision was to determine if I should stay here for the game itself or head to my actual seat and watch the game with Chris. I chose family over non-English speaking media (even though Pelé did speak English). On my way out of the row, I pleasantly acknowledged the purple beret wearing security guard and wished him good luck in securing the row—hopefully, no one more menacing than me would take advantage of his lack of attentiveness.

In a few minutes, I was now re-united with Chris at our seats, located on the corner behind one of the goals. Italy and Brazil battled to a 0-0 tie after regulation—a first for a World Cup Final. Now the two teams would engage in a penalty shoot-out, kicking at the goal where our seats were situated. Pure drama permeated the stadium, as a World Cup champion would be crowned within a couple of minutes—the tension was as thick as LA smog. Finally, Brazil won the shootout 3-2, after Italy's Roberto Baggio missed his game tying shootout kick when the ball sailed over the goal's crossbar. Pandemonium engulfed the stadium!

After watching the presentation of the World Cup trophy,

Chris and I walked back to our car, parked about a mile away. On the way, we stopped into a retail store called Heidi's Place, which sold sweatshirts, sweatpants and other similar merchandise that would be totally inappropriate for this toasty day. Perusing all the merchandise, we noticed the person at the back of the store by the cash register was none other than Heidi Fleiss—the notorious madame of Hollywood. Who would think that a madame would sell clothing such as sweatpants and sweatshirts—maybe her other customers, who were looking for some legal exercise. Before we departed the store, Chris, once again with his trusty camera, asked me if I wanted my picture taken with Heidi. I declined for several reasons, not least of which was I might need to get in touch with Robert Shapiro, again, to defend me if my wife saw such a compromising photograph.

LESSON LEARNED:

You never know who may have access to tickets and if you have a relative (wife, uncle, parent, third cousin), it may be to your advantage to inquire about a potential ticket—months in advance—for an event you seek to attend. And if you have the time to arrive at the event, long before the game itself commences, be sure to scout out prospective opportunities that allow you special access to the players, broadcasters, celebrities, etc. And again, it's a recurring theme—the access you seek may be provided by someone who is a bit sleepy and, yet, entrusted to maintain a modicum of security, preventing others—but not necessarily you—from encroaching on prohibited areas.

THE SUMMER OLYMPICS
1996

The 1996 Summer Olympics were held in Atlanta and presented a unique opportunity for me. The only other times a summer Olympics were in the US dated back to 1932 and 1984, both times, in Los Angeles. But now, I had a chance to view the summer games in the US–seeing a combination of patriotism and athleticism. Additionally, this would also be a moment to experience an international event that could be shared with family.

Alan, my cousin who is previously mentioned, now lived in Atlanta and, once again, agreed to host me in his home, with his wife, Mamie, and their two daughters. Also, my son, Patrick, who was seven years old at the time, would be joining me for some of the spectacular events.

Getting tickets to the Olympics was through a national

application process, and for the most part, were fairly easy to purchase for most of the events. The Olympics take place over a 17-day period and I planned to attend during the second week–boxing, weightlifting, volleyball, track & field were the events I wanted to see and they would take place the second half of the Olympics. Several weeks before the Olympics started, I was notified my tickets had been filled for all the above events, except for the boxing finals, which I figured could be attained with a little ingenuity once I was in Atlanta for the games.

I made my flight arrangements so that I would witness the weightlifting and volleyball with my cousin and then attend the two later track & field night events with my son. It all seemed like a solid plan–until disaster struck. During the first week of the Olympics, there was a massive bomb explosion at Centennial Olympic Park, a major congregation area in the Olympic Village. This was, potentially, an act of terrorism and posed a threat to the safety of spectators for future events.

I reconsidered not going for a fleeting moment, before quickly concluding that the probability of such an act repeating itself was less than my winning a gold medal in the Decathlon. Off to Atlanta and the summer Olympics I went!

The first event I attended was weightlifting, featuring some of the biggest and, clearly, strongest, men on earth– none of whom were my relatives, for obvious reasons. I saw a number of world records broken and only fantasized what it would be like to have the strength of such behemoths–especially, as I was weighing in at a prodigious weight in the 150 pound category. The following day, Alan and I saw some rather dull volleyball matches that merit no further discussion.

Patrick arrived a few days later and we saw two fantastic Track and Field events in the evening with 80,000 people in attendance. The highlight of the two nights was seeing Michael Johnson winning the 200 meters with his gold shoes in a record-breaking and electrifying 19.32 seconds–the crowd was shocked at this spectacular and memorable performance.

The following day, we intended to see the Boxing finals–an event where I would need to buy our tickets from a scalper, since this was one of the most in demand tickets and one that I had not been selected by the lottery. So, I needed two things–cash and a ticket seller. Using the ATM machine for the first time and holding up that line for what must have seemed like an eternity for those behind me, I received my $300 cash to buy two tickets. Shortly thereafter, I met a scalper who offered to sell me two tickets, located about 40 rows from the ring, a pretty good vantage point for the money I was willing to spend.

Once we were seated, before any matches started, the crowd broke into wild applause–Muhammad Ali walked into the arena and sat in the first row by the ring. His presence was a sensational surprise to everyone and an inspiration to the American boxers–who, unfortunately, needed more than his presence for inspiration.

For the first several matches, no American emerged victorious and, by that time, the crowd was becoming anxious with the futile results. Also, Patrick was getting bored, too, and began re-arranging the Olympic pins on his hat. While he was having difficulty putting one of the pins on his hat, he started to cry, asking me for help. Here I am at the Olympic boxing finals, trying to figure out how to attach various Olympic pins to my son's hat, paying no attention to the ring. All of a sudden, the crowd burst into thunderous applause–another American, David Reid, who was losing badly, had just knocked out his opponent, to win a gold medal! The only excitement of the afternoon and Patrick and I both missed it–consumed with attaching Olympic pins to a hat–so much for the painful pins!

On the final night, we were treated to a pass, allowing us into the NBC guest party at the Ritz Hotel in Buckhead. We managed to meet a few celebrities and especially enjoyed talking with Bob Costas, who was a major contributor on the Olympic broadcasts. The next day, we boarded our flight to Chicago. We had a great time with my cousin, watched some unbelievable Olympic events safely (no other acts of terrorism occurred) and had many terrific memories.

LESSON LEARNED:

Even for an event that happens every four years and has worldwide appeal, tickets can, unexpectedly, be fairly easy to acquire. As long as one prepares for the ticket lottery system, you can be assured of getting tickets to many of the most popular events. And for those where you are not selected, it is pretty easy to buy a ticket from a scalper at a reasonable cost. And one final note, if you're attending a top event with your child, expect to be interrupted and distracted at the most inopportune time—when one of your American athletes has just won a gold medal.

On a more serious note, with security becoming more of an issue at sporting events, although the threat of some terrorist act will always exist, it often is blown out of proportion—do your homework and, if it's prudent, take the calculated risk and go!

For years, attending a World Heavyweight Championship bout seemed to be one of the ultimate events to attend–it featured glad handing, waiting to be seen celebrities, well-choreographed pageantry, and, obviously, the pinnacle of machismo–two modern day gladiators, who would contend for a world title of manliness that would be decided in less than two hours. And so, in the early part of 1997, it was announced that Mike Tyson and Evander Holyfield would fight their second bout (Holyfield won the first fight) in June at the MGM Hotel in Las Vegas. Immediately, I made my flight arrangements and hotel reservation, staying at Las Vegas's finest–Treasure Island, where some of the guests represented a combination of trailer park cast offs, gang bangers and their significant others. How could I not feel more at home. The hotel was hardly a treasure, but I did feel like I was on a new cultural island.

Once again, all I needed was a ticket. Ironically, in May, I was flying home from Columbia, Missouri and ran into Wayne Newton, his wife and bodyguard at the airport, checking into my flight. Wayne had been performing in Branson, about 30 miles away. Our interaction resulted from their "entourage" wanting to be upgraded to first class, where I had a seat. After the gate agent described the Newton family situation, and because there were not enough seats in first class to accommodate both Wayne and his wife, I volunteered my first class seat for a small ransom (from the airline).

Having volunteered my seat and gaining a position of some leverage, I asked for a favor, in return, from the Newton entourage. I quickly approached their bodyguard, who introduced himself as "Bear"–fitting for his body size. After exchanging pleasantries, I confirmed that Wayne was quite a celebrity and wielded great influence in Las Vegas. Being the loyal bodyguard that "Bear" was (and not knowing the purpose of our conversation), he quickly acknowledged that his boss was not only influential in Las Vegas–he "owned" the town. That reply could not have been more pleasing to my ear!

At this point, I explained my situation of needing a ticket to the upcoming Tyson-Holyfield fight. Little did I know, "Bear" was a boxing aficionado and had attended many championship bouts over the years, dating back to Muhammad Ali. "Bear" mentioned that the upcoming June rematch would be the most in demand fight ticket since the first Ali-Frazier fight, 25 years earlier, but offered to take my business card and "would call" me if he had a line on a ticket. After giving him my card, I asked "Bear" for his phone number–just in case he lost my contact information (accidentally, of course). "Bear" would regret sharing his information (which was accurate) with me for the next two months. And once "Bear" found me sitting beside him on the plane for the next hour back to Chicago, while the Newtons were in first class, he was apoplectic—the last thing he wanted—or needed!

Religiously, I called "Bear" every other week until the fight. Surprisingly, he actually answered his phone or returned my call. Each time we spoke, he was very encouraging and, then, the week before the fight, "Bear" mentioned he did not have an actual ticket for me, but would be able to get me a "floater" pass, which allowed me to roam around the arena during the entire evening, while all of the fights happened. The week of the fight, "Bear" requested I call him that Friday (the fight being the next day—Saturday) when I arrived in Las Vegas, so we could coordinate arrangements to pick up and deliver the pass.

Well, after placing numerous phone calls, "Bear" became the invisible "Bear" that Friday. This disappearing act did not take me by total surprise, so I was prepared to buy a ticket from a scalper that night before the fight. Roaming around the MGM Hotel, there were plenty of tickets being scalped—but they were going for anywhere from $500-$2000 each—above my $400 budget. Finally, I came across a scalper who had a nose bleeder for my price. However, as you might imagine, I was concerned that the ticket was counterfeit, a normal practice at popular events. After verifying the ticket was legitimate with the person at the Will Call window, I exchanged my cash for the ticket—now, I could relax Friday night and Saturday, until the big event!

Before I describe the fight experience, it is worthwhile to provide some details of the Championship Fight scene in Las Vegas—both at my luxurious Treasure Island Hotel and the MGM Hotel.

Walking around the Treasure Island, and spending a little

time in the elevators, I was shocked to see the number of women who were in rather provocative attire, but not engaging in the world's oldest profession. These women, who were guests of someone, but not with them, would refer to their "guy" as "being in prison," "going to prison" or "getting out of prison." They talked about their guy and prison like many other women talked about their guy and his job–quite a cultural contrast. A renowned Chicago sports journalist described the women at the fight as "having more tattoos than the average prison inmate"–an understatement. And remember, this was 1997–long before tattoos became the common form of self-expression it is today.

At 7 pm that Saturday night, I was on my way from the Treasure Island to the MGM, with ticket in hand. Hoping to gain a better seat than my nose- bleed location, I wore my trusty navy blue blazer. Walking to the arena through the MGM was a little taste of stardom, as the hallways to the fight area were lined with people looking to catch a glimpse of the many "rich and famous" attending this significant event. I'm not sure they thought the guy with the fashionable blue blazer was a celebrity, but I was laughing to myself, walking past all of the gaping fans–my 15 minutes of fame (if that's what you call it).

I arrived at one of the preliminary bouts and found a seat about three rows from the ring. Real celebrities were in attendance–John F. Kennedy, Jr., Rodney Dangerfield, Shaq amongst others. I watched a number of fights before getting kicked out of my seat. Finally, the announcer broadcast that the World Championship fight would begin in 10 minutes and for everyone to take his or her seat. I was now resigned to sit in my nose bleed–until, as I was walking from the ring, I noticed one unoccupied chair in the 10th row, no less. I made my way to that seat and sat down, asking the guy next to me if the seat was taken.

He answered, "Yes, by you—because my guest just called to say he wouldn't be able to make the fight"—lady luck struck, once again. In front of me sat Tiger Woods, who had just won his first Masters and Paul Reiser, a comedy star in his own right. The face value of the ticket was $2000—who knows how much people paid for these seats. I paid $400—a pretty fair deal.

The fight was memorable because of its outrageous conclusion. Mike Tyson, after biting Evander Holyfield's ear for the second time, was disqualified! A riot in the stands ensued for about 10 minutes. The riot consisted of guys, who were from both Holyfield's and Tyson's camps and were big, mean, and ready to brawl. They made the real fighters look like choirboys. I was most happy they were on the opposite side of the ring and about 50 rows from where I was sitting—but where I would have been sitting, if I had sat where my actual ticket was assigned!

Walking out of the arena, after the fight was stopped in the 3rd round, I happened to be standing next to Tiger Woods. Not one to miss a chance to mingle with a sports celebrity, I casually asked him to sign my ticket stub. He responded with a dismissive "I'll sign it later"—as if we were partying back in his suite later that night—which we did not. The line proceeded for a bit, until it halted for a few minutes, prompting me to ask Tiger, "if now was a better time to autograph my ticket"—hey, it was later than the last time I asked him the same question. Well, not late enough, because his buddy interceded on his behalf, saying Tiger didn't like to be disturbed at these events. I respected his wishes—finally—and decided to stay in the arena as everyone else was departing.

To put my encounter with Tiger into perspective, the previous year, at a black-tie event I attended, Muhammad Ali was the guest of honor. Knowing this in advance and wearing the suggested tuxedo attire, I came well prepared for the opportunity–bringing a grocery bag full of boxing gloves and the famous photo of him with Sonny Liston into the event ballroom–talk about style. As the evening unfolded, Ali, patiently, signed every autograph seeker's item(s), including my grocery bag of paraphernalia. Here he was, a worldwide icon, not just a sports figure, with his debilitating Parkinson's disease, signing hundreds of autographs and posing for pictures. Tiger, on the hand, had just won his first major at his worldly 21 years of age, and could not be bothered for a fleeting moment, to sign even one autograph.

After my cordial encounter with Tiger, I managed to get to the ring where Ronnie Lott–the famous 49er, was hanging out with the fight judge, Mills Lane, who officiated the memorable bout. Splattered with blood, Mills actually agreed to sign my ticket stub before I retreated from the arena to the MGM casino–the world's largest. As I was watching some blackjack players in a cordoned off area, who were playing with only $1000 and $5000 chips (and piles of them), gun shots rang out in the casino. Hysterically, everyone hid in the pits or under the tables for their safety. Pandemonium reigned for 10 minutes, until the shots finally ceased. Again, this was quite a different experience for someone who grew up in a neighborhood where the only shots came from their new television set.

Now that this second act of craziness subsided, I quickly headed to my hotel room and promptly called United Airlines to see if they could get me on the first flight back to Chicago the next morning–I was in no mood to wait for my afternoon flight and see what the next extraordinary experience would bring. The surreal world of bitten ears, riots, and gunshots had provided me with enough excitement to last a lifetime. Fortunately, I was able to catch United's first flight back to Chicago that Sunday morning–my rather mundane life was a welcome relief from the chaos of Las Vegas that weekend.

LESSON LEARNED:

Expect to have someone's promise to you broken and prepare a contingency plan. And when you shell out huge dollars for a marquee event ticket to someone who you do not know, make sure you verify the legitimacy of the ticket, which can be done very easily. Before buying the ticket, just approach one of the people scanning tickets to ensure that yours is authentic—this could save you hundreds of dollars. Oh, and once you begin witnessing riots and hearing gunshots, it's a sign to end the evening and count your blessings that you live in an entirely different world—hopefully.

These two events are combined because they both entailed me taking my son to them and are US Open events, coincidentally. In 2000, my son and I attended the US Open Tennis Finals, as a stroke of luck. A week before the finals, I was offered two tickets, by a consultant, who was trying to cultivate a relationship with my employer, another investment firm where I was working.

Patrick and I took the first morning flight out of Chicago for LaGuardia and arrived in NYC, where the US Open Tennis tournament is held, around noon. For the next several hours, we walked around Flushing Meadows, watching Chris Evert give lessons to a bunch of corporate sponsors. Additionally, we saw both Pete Sampras and Marat Safin, the two US Open finalists, practice for about an hour before the match began.

The match started a little after 5 pm and was relatively uneventful, except for the fact that Safin, the underdog, beat Sampras in a rather methodical manner, winning in three straight sets. The match was over by 7:30, allowing us to get to LaGuardia for our 10 pm flight—which was delayed a couple of hours. We were home shortly after midnight—a quick but enjoyable day in NYC at the finals of the US Open Tennis tournament.

Three years later in 2003, Patrick and I attended the US Open Golf tournament, played at Olympia Fields Country Club in Olympia Fields, a southern Chicago suburb—just north of Florida. It took us about two hours to drive to the tournament from our north suburban home on a sweltering day, where the temperatures hovered in the high 90's.

At this time, I was with a large national bank, an institution that knew how to entertain. At the US Open, the bank provided a tent for its many clients. So, Patrick and I, on this sweltering day, watched a number of players—Tiger Woods, et al., before seeking the cool air conditioning of the tent—accompanied by food, beverages and TVs. You may get the picture—the tent (not the golf tournament) was the day's highlight—oh, yes, Jim Furyk won the tournament.

Although we were there for the supposed climactic Sunday final round, we left before the tournament's conclusion, so that we would make it back for a home cooked meal by my mother-in-law. You know the tournament lacks excitement when it's pre-empted by your mother-in-law—regardless of her culinary capability.

LESSON LEARNED:

The US Open Golf tournament was an easy ticket to acquire, as a result of the lack of suspense and overall viewing experience. Although the grounds of the golf course may be lovely, your time and wallet would be better spent walking in the park and dropping a c-note in the cup of the closest panhandler. The US Open Tennis Tournament—there is certainly a buzz in NYC and you can see every aspect of the match—even if you are in the nose-bleeds, which we were. If you enjoy tennis or appreciate athleticism, you would not regret attending this event. Tickets are pretty available and fairly affordable.

It has been said that the Masters is the hardest ticket to get in sports. Whether or not that claim is true, the tournament is one of the most majestic events to attend. It is played at the ultra-prestigious Augusta National in early April, just as the Georgia azaleas begin to bloom. Not a blade of grass is too long or short, not a weed rears its head and no "patron" would think of littering even a stick of gum—for this is the cathedral of golf!

Prior to 2006, I had the fortune of attending the practice rounds of the Masters in both 2000, by lottery, and 2005, through a neighbor. The beauty of the practice rounds, as opposed to the tournament itself, is that you get closer to the players, because the crowds are smaller, and are allowed to use your video or regular camera—cell phones are prohibited. Memorializing the grounds, players and Augusta environment is a precious way to treasure such a wonderful experience.

In 2006, I was given the privilege of inviting two guests and my wife to join me for the Saturday and Sunday rounds. At the time, I worked for a significant financial services firm that catered to a "Who's Who" of entrepreneurs, corporate titans, celebrities and overall wealthy families.

The firm was able to host many guests at the Masters because its top two Board directors were Augusta club members. Consequently, we had six guest tickets each day, plus member passes, which allowed us access to the magnificent Trophy Room and the hallowed clubhouse–where only members are allowed during the tournament.

My wife and I flew down to the Masters that Friday night, April 7th, via Atlanta, and drove the 120 miles to Augusta, where my employer had rented a beautiful house for us and our guests. After a filling Southern meal that nearly caused early heart failure, we went to bed to make sure we were ready for the big event–Saturday's Masters.

Once we finished eating a hearty breakfast, consisting of the always nutritious grits and other cholesterol enhancing foods, our driver took us to the course on a gloomy day that wasn't very promising. In fact, after a couple of hours, the course would close due to a thunderstorm. This was not much of a problem, as it afforded us plenty of extra time to buy loads of Masters logo merchandise, setting the stage for a memorable Sunday experience.

Sunday was as beautiful as Saturday was ugly–not a cloud in the sky and the temperatures were in the mid 70's. After a few hours on the course, my wife and I needed to use the facilities, and since we were near the clubhouse, and had the appropriate member badge, that's where we were headed. While I was upstairs in the men's locker room, my wife was downstairs, by the front door entrance, talking to another member, presumably. All of a sudden, at the same time my wife turned away from the front door, a rather imposing man entered the clubhouse with his head transfixed ahead—neither aware of the other person. As such, they collided and my wife ended on the clubhouse floor.

Rising to her feet and dusting herself off, she noticed the person, who virtually body slammed her to the floor, was none other than Tiger Woods. He apologized profusely and asked how he could help her, extending his hand for further assistance lifting her from the floor. My wife said she was fine, only to realize the following day a prodigious purple bruise, the size of a grapefruit, on her thigh. Tiger always had a unique way of picking up women—if only he had been so cordial to me in Las Vegas.

Once we avoided bumping into Tiger Woods for the rest of the day, we watched the tournament from each of the holes for a couple of hours, before settling on the bend of the magnificent par 5, 13th and the par 3, 16th. The day was a sensational experience, although we had to leave before the tournament's completion. Arriving at the airport a couple of hours later to catch our flight, we saw Phil Mickelson win his second green jacket, on television. Nonetheless, attending the Masters is more about the experience and event's grandeur than watching a particular golfer capture the championship.

In an interesting postscript, several months later, my employer hosted a client luncheon in Chicago, where the Board member, whose pass I had used at The Masters, spoke and welcomed the guests. While the crowd was mingling, I re-introduced myself to him, expressing my appreciation for a very memorable Masters experience, recounting the Tiger Woods incident in the clubhouse. At that point, the Board member nodded his head and acknowledged that he had heard there were people who wore his badge and used it to gain access to the clubhouse. He proceeded to say that only members were allowed in the clubhouse, even if you were using a member's badge.

Knowing his badges were used inappropriately by fellow hosts (like my wife and me) and guests, the Board member discussed this situation with his cousin, another member of Augusta, to see if they should bring the "transgression" to the attention of Augusta's Board. They decided to keep the story quiet, which could have resulted in him being suspended or expelled from the club, if it was made public.

Now you know why I had a habit of changing companies every five years or so—I had an interesting way of making strong impressions with the company's top executives— what a way to build a career in your first year with a firm— almost getting the Board member expelled from Augusta— the most prestigious club in America!

LESSONS LEARNED:

I was lucky on each visit to the Masters. The first time, I was one of 300 people who was selected in a Chicago District Golf Association lottery for the practice round; the second time, my neighbor gave me his ticket to the practice round because he had a business commitment and my third time, my firm's senior managing director thought enough of me to let me attend the Masters with my wife and client.

Since attending Augusta is a once in a lifetime thrill, it is important that you walk every hole, so that you can appreciate the magnificent grounds in their entirety. The grandeur and beauty are more breathtaking than what is captured on television and the landscape has more undulation, which requires a level of fitness during your walk.

Once again, pushing the envelope gave my wife the unexpected run in with a golf celebrity and almost got the Board member expelled and me fired. Always keep your eyes open and don't hesitate to enter the applicable Masters lottery, as many states' golf associations do conduct them. So enter early and often—like a good Chicagoan voter.

In the event you are representing the Board member of your company, to avoid potential career suicide, make sure you are following the rules and regulations of the particular event (or club in this instance)—although that decision may not lead to as many bizarre stories.

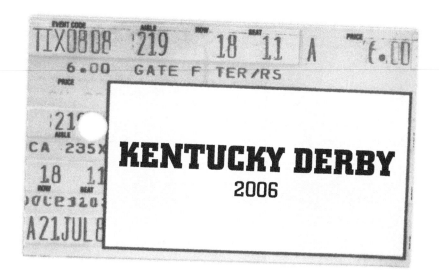

TIX0808 219 18 11 A 6.00
6.00 GATE F TER/RS
21
CA 235X
18 11
ACE320
A21JUL

KENTUCKY DERBY
2006

Once again, I had the fortune of experiencing this event in grand style, as a result of my employer, who was a sponsor of the Breeder's Cup, which allowed us special treatment at the Derby itself. And, also again, I attended this event with clients and prospects.

Before attending the Derby itself, once we arrived in Louisville that Friday, we had a private tour of the nation's premier horse farm, Claiborne, and one of Kentucky's bourbon distilleries, Maker's Mark, both located near Lexington. On this particular day at Claiborne, where the legendary Secretariat is buried, we actually witnessed a foal being delivered; a rarity, because it happened in the daytime and, also, because it was outside, in full view of us and our guests. And speaking of the tour of the bourbon distillery, if they had not provided so many samples, I would be able to provide more details of the experience than this—which now will conclude my description of that tour.

Finally, on Saturday, we entered Churchill Downs around noon, where we had a private suite on the infield at the finish line—one of the finest viewing areas at the track. Not only was it easy for us to order our preferred beverages—and the popular Mint Juleps—there was plenty of food available throughout the entire day. Most importantly, placing a bet was easy—we literally walked outside our suite, strolled to the nearby betting window, and made our wager. This was considerably more civilized than waiting in line for 15 minutes, between races, with people whose last beverage was decorating their favorite t-shirt.

During this Derby Day, about 157,000 people (the second largest Derby crowd ever) were in Churchill Downs to view the 10 races before the actual Derby race. Essentially, 35,000 have reserved seats in the grandstands and the remaining 100,000+in the infield—where the level of intoxication rivals that of a Harley-Davidson rendezvous in Sturgis. Our infield suite belied the typical style in which people in the infield participate in the Derby—the average infield attendee is younger than 30, barely has $30 in their pockets and, by the time they leave Churchill Downs, has consumed 30 beers—or their favorite libation. Their biggest claim to fame is making it to Louisville and back home in one piece—and remembering how they did it.

Our suite was filled with quasi royalty—people whose net worth was at least $10 million—some of whom were worth over $1 billion. Despite the extreme affluence of our guests, everyone just let the day evolve, let their hair down, and had a great time—regardless of their skill in picking horses or lack of hair.

As the actual Derby race is about to begin, "the most exciting two minutes in sports" is filled with palpitating anticipation. Fortunately, despite my tendency to avoid gambling, I actually placed an obligatory (and paltry) $5 on the right horse—Barbaro. Barbaro got out of the gate, quickly, and from there took a commanding lead, which was never relinquished. In fact, although Barbaro's time was a bit off the record of Secretariat's, he won the race by 6 ½ lengths—the largest margin in 60 years. His victory paid the winning bettors $14, enough to cover the cost of the whopping tips I left during the weekend.

This historical Derby victory would soon be overshadowed by the tragic misfortune at the next race; The Preakness, where Barbaro stumbled out of the gate and broke his ankle. There were several months of medical attention given to Barbaro in hopes that he could recover. Pathetically, no procedure was successful, resulting in him being put to sleep. Barbaro was a spectacular horse, whose fame was fleeting. His name and record will forever be etched in the memories of millions of horse racing fans.

LESSON LEARNED:

History repeated itself, as I was lucky to have my business connection give me access to this special event. So, how do you want to experience the Derby? If you are up for sharing the day with over 100,000 people—in the infield—a ticket is as easy to buy as contacting a disease while watching the race from this area. For those of you interested in a Roman bacchanalia, this is the place for you.

If, on the other hand, you are looking for more civility, viewing the race from the grandstands is a wonderful way to spend a few hours at Churchill Downs. Tickets for this area are still available outside of the racetrack and are much more reasonably priced than through a broker. Of course, if your company is entertaining clients at the Derby, you get the best value—tickets are free (quite a deal, given that suites go for over $10,000.)

Actually, one of the biggest challenges of attending the Derby is securing a hotel room. Rooms in Louisville for Derby weekend are sold out a year in advance, so you may have to resort to booking accommodations in either Lexington, about 75 miles away, or Indianapolis, about 115 miles away. Regardless, the trip will be worth the experience; you'll have plenty of memories to share and, hopefully, a few extra bucks in your pocket.

The venerable and world renowned Ryder Cup is played every two years, alternating between US and Europe soil. Golf fans revere this classic contest between the top American and European golfers, as the most anticipated golf event in the world—during those biennial years.

In 2012, the Ryder Cup was played at Medinah Country Club, located about 20 miles from my north suburban home. For months leading up to this event that had never been played in Chicago, tickets were capturing their usual 3-4 times face value, as Chicagoans (and other Americans) sweated the thought of missing out on this opportunity to personally experience one of the most patriotic sports contests. In fact, if normal tickets were expensive, corporate tents were selling for tens of thousands of dollars—sometimes as much as $100,000 for the entire week.

The Ryder Cup features 12 golfers from each team and after 2012's first two Ryder Cup days–Friday and Saturday–the US had a significant lead of 10-6, needing only 4 ½ more points to win the Cup. Certainly, by most expert's views, the final matches on Sunday would see the US retake the Cup back from the Europeans. Since I had only seen a Ryder Cup practice round in 2006, when the contest was in Boston, I thought attending the final day in Chicago would be historical and memorable–which it was (unfortunately, for the wrong reasons.)

Procuring a ticket proved to be quite easy, as I purchased a pass, good for the International Tent, in the parking lot at Arlington Park, where shuttle buses were running to Medinah, for $150–only $30 over face value and considerably lower than the $500 they were fetching weeks beforehand.

Better yet, adopting the "act like you belong" attitude, I decided to forgo the International Tent (where all items were for purchase) for the International Media Hospitality tent, where I was able to "act" my way into the tent and enjoy a more intimate experience with any kind of food and beverage. I always believe that watching a sporting event is more enjoyable after consuming a nice hearty meal with a couple of beverages–especially, when it's on the house, as it always is for the media.

That Sunday was a beautiful September day, and Medinah was host to another large crowd of American and European golf fans–approximately 45,000 fans entered the Medinah gates and witnessed what would become either a choke job by the Americans or a courageous rally by the Europeans–depending on your view.

As with any golf tournament, you are faced with a couple of decisions–do you situate yourself at a particular hole and watch the respective pairings play throughout the day, or do you decide to follow one or two pairings, walking hole to hole. Unfortunately, in either case, you cannot see what is happening, first hand, on the other holes and have to rely on either a gimmicky for rent radio, broadcasting the hole by hole results of the pairings or watch the leader board, providing the somewhat delayed updates.

I decided to perch myself behind the par three 13th and watched one American pairing after the next succumb to their European competitors. The European team won the first four matches of the day, tying the score 10-10, before the Americans rallied to take a 13-12 lead, with three matches remaining. But Europe won the final two matches and halved the third to win 14 ½- 13 ½ in dramatic fashion.

The weather was magnificent, the media hospitality tent extremely hospitable, the grounds were pristine, the crowd was politely raucous and patriotic—unfortunately, from an American's perspective, the US's team results were just the opposite.

LESSON LEARNED:

The best part about attending golf matches is walking around the magnificently manicured grounds of the course. However, from the perspective of a true sports fan, golf is the worst sporting event to attend, because you only see about 10% of the actual action—at most. In particular, at the Ryder Cup, where there are only a limited number of matches being played, the crowd size on each hole is huge— far larger than at a typical golf tournament, where you have golfers on each of the 18 holes (as opposed to only 12 holes at a time at the Ryder Cup.)

The beauty of the Ryder Cup is that the crowds are rowdier, and you have a chance to participate in a fun, patriotic exercise—it does not draw the typical European hooligan, who is smashing one pint after another on someone's head.

Once more, when looking to buy a ticket, don't believe the pre-event ticket hype—be patient and you'll get your admission ticket for a very reasonable price.

A ticket stub reading:

TIX0808 219 18 11 A €.00
6.00 GATE F TER/RS
PRICE
21
AISLE
CA 235X
18 11
ROW SEAT
0CE316
A21JUL8

STANLEY CUP
FINALS
2013

Although I had attended the 1992 Stanley Cup Finals, when the Chicago Blackhawks played the Pittsburgh Penguins, I almost dismiss that experience because the Hawks lost in four straight games—I witnessed the final loss and the Penguins skating around the ice in Chicago Stadium, hoisting the Cup. And then in 2010, when the Blackhawks were in the Finals again, business trip logistics prevented me from flying to Philadelphia to see the Hawks win their first Stanley Cup in 49 years.

So, when the Hawks were tied with the Boston Bruins in the 2013 Finals, two games to two games, they played game five on a Saturday at the United Center, which the Hawks won 3-1. Game six, potentially the game when the Hawks could win the Stanley Cup, would be played that following

Monday night in Boston. I had no ticket, lodging or flights, as of 10 pm that Saturday evening—so I needed to get to work quickly, because this would be my opportunity to see the Hawks win the Stanley Cup—LIVE!

Later that Saturday night, I immediately booked my airfare to Boston on an 11:35 am flight for Monday, arriving in Boston at 2:30 that afternoon—about five hours before game time. Using the ever-present handy frequent flyer miles helped reduce the expense of this upcoming adventure. Next, I attempted to make a reservation at over 35 hotels, all of which were sold out for some reason (not having to do with the hockey game). Fortunately, I was able to use a reciprocal club of mine, the Union Club, located 15 minutes from Logan Airport and a 15 minute walk from the Bruins home venue—TD Garden—a perfect location.

Again, the final step was to land a ticket, which actually ended up being fairly easy—inexplicably. Talking to brokers that Sunday, throughout the day, and looking at StubHub, a source I had never used in the past, there were over 2700 tickets available for game six of the Stanley Cup Finals. Tickets ranged from $250 for 300 level seats to $800 for seats in the first 15 rows of the corners. By Sunday night, tickets were still plentiful (2400) and were dropping in price—I finally bought one on StubHub in the 10th row by the face-off circle where the Blackhawks would be shooting twice for $550—a steal, especially when compared to tickets similar in location that had sold at the United Center in game five for over $2000 each. And given the marvels of modern technology, I put the $550 ticket charge on my Visa and was able to print the ticket right there by my home office desk—there was no need to spend time picking it up in Boston the next day—a nice time saver.

So, Monday morning was going to be the start of, after much reflection, my most memorable sporting experience of all time. I packed my son's authentic Patrick Kane jersey, but wore my reliable navy blue sport coat, blue button Oxford shirt and khaki pants—my reliable sporting event uniform. The plane left on time, which was fortunate, as shortly thereafter, weather at O'Hare became terrible and hundreds of flights were cancelled. I was now on my way to Boston and would view game six of the Stanley Cup Finals—in person!

I landed in Boston around 2:30, took a taxi to the Union Club, went to my $150 a night room, and was greeted by what you would expect for $150—a small bed, a window unit air conditioner and no bathroom, which was located down the hall (but assigned only to my room—luxury at its best). After conducting some business on the phone, I grabbed a quick bite to eat and got ready for the game.

The biggest decision was whether I should wear my son's Patrick Kane jersey. I decided against doing so, thinking that if the Hawks won the game and Stanley Cup, and I was walking back to the Union Club, alone at night, wearing the jersey, I could find myself in a rather challenging situation, that might provoke a Bruin fan or two, or three or four. I would not be excited to face such a potential encounter with my face, especially since I would already be filled with excitement from the Hawks winning the Stanley Cup. Little did I know what the positive ramifications of this decision would be later that evening.

I arrived at the TD Garden by 7 pm for the 8 pm game. Once I was there, I hung around a group of Hawks fans that congregated near the Hawks bench, where the team eventually took the ice. As the teams started their pregame skate, the Garden resembled nothing less than a modern day Coliseum, with music blaring and the Bruins' bellicose fans ready to assist their team's attempt at intimidating the Blackhawks.

The Bruins totally dominated the first period, scoring just one and the only goal, which was fortunate for the

Blackhawks, given their lackluster play. Soon after the second period began, Hawks' team captain, Jonathan Toews, scored to tie the game, which is where the game stood after the first two periods. Period three continued to deliver the same intensity as the previous five games. With a little more than seven minutes to play, the Bruins scored again and bedlam ensued at the Garden. At this point, it looked like the series would return to Chicago for a decisive seventh and another ulcer producing game. But let's not come to conclusions too quickly.

Shortly after the Bruins scored, the Hawks struck luck and found themselves on a power play. Unfortunately, their luck did not last during their one man advantage, as they, once again, did not capitalize on this potential game tying opportunity. With about one and a half minutes remaining in the game, the Hawks pulled their goalie, Corey Crawford, to add another shooter, who, hopefully, would score the tying goal. Literally, within seconds of pulling Crawford, the Hawks scored a miraculous goal–the tying tally coming from Bryan Bickell, on a sensational pass from Jonathan Toews. Naturally, the wildly outnumbered Hawks fans erupted in joy, thinking they might now see their team win the Stanley Cup–but almost assuredly requiring another overtime period.

Exactly 17 seconds later, the Hawks did the impossible–they scored again–this time Dave Boland scored on a rebound from the slap shot of Johnny Oduya! Hawks fans–and I–were delirious–Bruins fans were comatose. This was the quickest turnaround in the history of a Stanley Cup Finals game. Now, it was the Bruins turn to pull their goalie to see if they could tie the game. Being shell shocked as they were, the Bruins could not mount much of an attack the last 60 nerve wrecking seconds of the game. Yes, the Hawks won the 2013 Stanley Cup in the most electrifying manner in the history of the Stanley Cup Finals!

Next came the customary handshakes between both teams and the Stanley Cup presentation to the Hawks, who, one by one, would skate around the rink with the Cup hoisted over their respective heads. There is no better way for a team to celebrate and be crowned their sport's champions!

After about 15 minutes of watching the post-game ceremonies, I would now experience another lifetime memory, as if watching my hometown hockey team win the Stanley Cup—in a dramatic 17 seconds—was not enough of a thrill.

I began to notice a number of people walking onto the ice, from the opposite side of the rink. Walking onto the ice looked like an interesting idea, so I quickly ran to that area on the concourse, but did not know the way down to the ice where the other people were entering the rink. Well, it just so happened that my confusion was also being experienced by others, too—in this case, people who were all wearing the same Hawks jersey, with the same number—#50. Introducing myself, this was the family of Corey Crawford (the Hawks goalie)—the parents, sister and brother, all of whom were livid that they had not found a way to get down on the ice to celebrate with their son and brother—plenty of "F-bombs" expressed by the family.

How could I not offer to help them get down on the ice, and personally accompany them—with the help of a security guard, of course (someone who actually did know the circuitous route downstairs and through the meandering hallways to get us on the ice). At this point, I was doing my best impression of being "Corey Crawford's uncle"—and a rather short one at that.

Of course, the way onto the ice was a bit more challenging than a brief walk—there were the ever-present security guards on the floor, adjacent to the rink, checking the credentials of families and friends, who would be celebrating with their Blackhawk player. In this case, each person would be wearing the "official" pink and yellow wristbands to prove they were a legitimate friend or family member. The only thing I had on my wrist was a watch–and it was blue. But, here again, you need to have a bit of guile. The inspections were quite haphazard and very undisciplined–much to my good fortune–and similar to other experiences I have had at noteworthy events. As they were asking a show of the wristband, I kept walking, with an apparent hearing disorder–all the while, wearing my favorite navy blue sport coat–lending me somewhat of an air of legitimacy–and certainly the best dressed member of the Crawford family (each of whom, of course, was wearing the required wristbands.)

As the Crawfords and I entered the ice, Corey immediately embraced his family and looked at me quizzically. I clearly was no family member, but all was well–I was on the ice, celebrating with all of the Hawks, their families and close friends–but just as a long-time fan! Thank God I was not wearing a Patrick Kane jersey–that would not have meshed too well with the Crawfords.

For the next hour, I would be taking video of the entire extravaganza. A few of the Hawks families even asked me to take pictures of their sons with them–in particular, Duncan Keith and Andrew Shaw. I was now using my photographic talents, limited as they were, to record these memorable moments for the Hawks themselves–that was the least I could do!

In the midst of my picture taking and video recording, I bumped into John McDonough, the Hawks President and a past business contact, and Pat Foley, the Hawks broadcaster, and a friend from high school. They seemed perplexed to see me on the ice–but this was no time to share my secrets and we just exchanged high fives and lots of laughs. About half an hour into my ice time, I began receiving phone messages and texts from friends in Chicago, letting me know they were following my whereabouts, captured on the local television stations' coverage of the on ice celebrations. Fortunately, I looked moderately official and was not caught performing some inappropriate or compromising gesture.

Finally, the Garden had enough of the Hawks and their family and friends' celebration and began ushering people off the ice and out of the arena. I finally got back to my room at the Union Club at 1:15 am, calling my son, Patrick, to inform him of the recent adventure. I had a 6 am flight that morning and a wake-up call at 4 am. Existing on less than 3 hours sleep was made possible only by such an adrenalin producing experience. This was an evening and an event that will never be topped!

LESSON LEARNED:

When your favorite team is in the final championship round in their respective sport, it likely is easier seeing them (and paying less for a ticket) in the city where the opposing team plays—especially, if that city is smaller than the one where you live. This is particularly true if your team's opponent is behind in the series, where the opponent's fans may have lost faith in their team, and, consequently, less likely to attend the, potentially, final game of the series—their lack of loyalty may be your good fortune.

Also, if you have even the most remote idea of going beyond the standard fan's seating arrangements—press box, on the field, court or ice, etc., leave your team jersey at home—that will only identify you as just another fan—not a clever fan, who is trying to look official and wants special access to official areas. Remember, get out your sport coat—preferably blue, and wear it proudly—you'll look the part, feel the part and, hopefully, be part of the real action with the press and players!

WORLD SERIES
—THE GRAND FINALE—
THE CUBS BECOME
WORLD CHAMPIONS
2016

Over the years, as I have recounted in these pages, I have been fortunate to experience, as a spectator, Chicago's sports teams winning their respective championships—the Bears winning the Super Bowl, the Bulls winning the James O'Brien trophy (aka the NBA Championship) and the Blackhawks winning the Stanley Cup. Although I have cheered for the White Sox, they were not my favorite baseball team in Chicago. So, when they won the World Series in 2005, I was rather indifferent. Conspicuous by its absence was none other than the beloved Cubs, who, up to 2016, had not won the World Series in 108 years—more than one very futile lifetime! That chapter of failure would now end—FINALLY!

With that as a backdrop, this closing segment will be

far lengthier than the others, appropriate for a number of reasons. First, let's recap the recent years of Cubs futility, to fully appreciate the significance of their World Series Championship.

In 1969, the team featured legends such as Ernie Banks, Billy Williams and Ron Santo, luminaries that shaped the Cubs fans support for many years. The Cubs, as an example that year, had representatives in each position on the field at the annual All-Star Game—a rarity! They led their division by nine games, as late as mid-August. Hopes for a Cubs pennant and, potentially, winning the World Series were sky high. Then the team began a colossal collapse that resulted in the New York Mets winning both the Pennant and, after, the World Series. Mets fans had only seven years to wait before their team won the Championship title—they were established in 1962, with an inauspicious season record of losing 121 games—winning only 40 games.

After suffering that heartbreak, it took the Cubs 15 more years to become a truly competitive team again, winning their division in 1984. During the playoffs against the San Diego Padres, they took a 2-0 game lead, before heading off to San Diego, needing only one more victory to clinch the Pennant and moving into the World Series.

The teams were tied in games 2-2, as the decisive 5th game was to be played. In game five, the Cubs took a quick lead. Hope was again very high, until Cubs first baseman, Leon Durham, committed an error that eventually led to the Padres game- winning rally. Once more, futility struck and the Cubs missed winning the Pennant and going to the World Series.

But, despite all of their misfortune, up till that point, and the so-called curse of The Billy Goat, which started in 1945, when the team lost to the Detroit Tigers in seven games in the World Series, the most infamous year of bad luck was in 2003. That year, the Cubs boasted young, outstanding pitchers, such as Mark Prior and Kerry Wood, and a prolific home run hitter, Sammy Sosa—who became infamous in his own right, as an accused steroid user.

Once again, the Cubs were in the playoffs to win the Pennant and had a commanding 3-1 game lead against the Florida Marlins, playing games six and seven at Wrigley Field. Pitching for the Cubs on game six was Mark Prior, their star, young pitcher. The Cubs took another lead and were winning 3-1, with one out in the top of the eighth inning—they needed only five more outs to win the Pennant and be back in the World Series!

Well, once more, the curse of the goat struck. At this point, the Marlins had a runner on first base, when the next batter, Luis Castillo, hit a fly ball down the left field foul line—no one could tell if it would remain in play or go into the stands. The Cubs' left fielder, Moises Alou, approached the left field foul line, where a wall separates the fans from the field. As he leaped to make the catch, with his glove over the wall, in foul territory, a fan stretched out his hands to grab the ball, thus interfering with Alou's attempt to make the catch. Who was this fan? Steve Bartman, the most beleaguered Cubs' fan.

After Alou was not able to make the catch, he stomped his feet in anger—yet, still no real problem, as the Cubs retained their lead. However, shortly thereafter, a ball was hit to the Cubs shortstop, Alex Gonzalez, who muffed a perfect double play opportunity—that's when the proverbial "wheels fell off." The Marlins went on to score eight runs and won game six, to set up the pivotal game seven match-up. Having attended game six, the depression that encompassed the field, fans and team was palpable. But, they still could win the Pennant, if they were able to regroup and win the final seventh game.

I also had tickets to game seven, and entering Wrigley Field was like attending a funeral, before the body was dead–they should have been passing out Xanax, because no consumption of beer could elevate the fans' hopes. Even though the Cubs took a small lead, the Marlins won the game and, eventually, the World Series (their second since 1997). Keep in mind, by this time, the Marlins had been a professional baseball team for only 12 years.

Then, in years 2008 and 2009, the Cubs made it to the playoffs and lost to both the Dodgers and the Diamondbacks, three straight games each year, without a victory–more infamy. At this point, the team's futility was legendary and known throughout the country (if not the world)–how could this infamous losing record be broken? Well, a change of ownership might do the trick–so, in October of 2009, the Cubs were sold to the Ricketts family, a family I had known since 2005, through a business relationship.

In particular, Tom Ricketts, the team's new CEO, and I had spent a fair amount of time together before his family purchased the team–my son and I took Tom and his son to the Bears Championship game in Soldier Field in 2006 and, ironically, I once took Tom and his sons to be MY guests at a Cubs game, where I was able to get them on the field, before the game, and their name on the iconic red Marquis outside the field (hey, I was just trying to whet his appetite for becoming the team's future owner–I guess you could say that Tom and his family outdid me, right?)

Additionally, Tom and I would have lunch once or twice a year. One lunch, specifically, was quite memorable, as it took place in the heart of the negation process. While we were dining at the University Club the summer of 2009, Tom received an urgent message on his phone regarding the family's potential purchase of the Cubs. Tom looked at me and said he was going to have to excuse himself, because the moment of truth was at hand and the deal was either going to happen or collapse, imminently. Here I was, lunching with Tom, and the future ownership of the team was going to be determined in very short order—always nice to witness history firsthand.

Anecdotally, when the Cubs were originally put up for sale, a number of investor groups were vying to be the top bidder. One group included a gentleman who I had known through a common connection at the Grammy's (although neither of us performed—just in case you were wondering.) During a meeting in his office, knowing that this gentleman was part of a group that was bidding on the Cubs, I mentioned that I thought a good way to diversify my investment portfolio would be to own a portion of the team. Looking straight at me, he said that he and his partners would welcome me to their syndicate—$10,000,000 a share. HMMM, I said, "was there a maximum number of shares I could buy." So, now that the issue of me becoming even a small investor was settled—and quickly—I resigned myself to at least know, potentially, the new owners.

After the Ricketts' purchase of the team became official, I continued to go to many Cubs games for a couple of years. However, as time went on, Tom became more entrenched with the team and we didn't have the same opportunity to get together as we once did, unfortunately.

All right, so now we are in 2016, and the Cubs are having a great year, winning over 100 games, and are the favorite to capture the World Series. On October 22nd, the Cubs beat the Los Angeles Dodgers and are headed to the World Series!!!

As one could imagine, the pent up demand for a ticket to see the Cubs in the World Series was monumental. Specifically, tickets for their first two home games were astronomical—as an example, box seats in the first few rows were fetching $25,000 each (how many did you want)? To just get into the park would run at least $2000. Since I had not had contact with Tom and the team for a few years, I would now be trying to get a ticket on my own. I passed on the first couple of home games—my good fortune because if

I had gone, I would have seen the Cubs lose and have paid a very high price.

So, for game five, the last game to be played at Wrigley Field for the Series, my son, Patrick (and his brother-in-law, Chris), and I made a game time decision, around noon, that Sunday to procure World Series tickets. We entered the Wrigley Field atmosphere at 4 pm, for the 7 pm game, without tickets, waiting to see how things would develop. Ticket prices were a fraction of what they were the previous two days–but still a large multiple (trying to use arithmetic terms now) of their face value. Loyal Cubs fans lost some of their loyalty and were in no mood to see the team, potentially, lose their third straight game–and be eliminated from the Series.

The three of us had a plan and relied on the advice of an old friend, who owned one of the largest ticket broker firms in Chicago. We met my broker friend a block away from Wrigley Field around 4 pm–ticket prices were hovering at about $1500 for standing room and $3000 for a decent, but not great seat. His advice–"sit tight and wait until 6 pm" when ticket prices will begin to decline appreciably. So, we just were patient and absorbed the whole atmosphere of buying a ticket to an event that was, reportedly, the hottest on sports record. We were spectators of the constant flow of buyers and sellers of these "hot" tickets–tickets that we wanted to buy–but did not need to buy. Most of the action was on Addison and Sheffield, where the streets were teeming with ticket brokers, scalpers, buyers and just plain onlookers, who wanted to be part of the scene, although they couldn't afford to be in the park. Everyone was praying that this game would resurrect the hopes of the Cubs, who could not afford to lose and be eliminated. The crowd was, actually, pretty orderly–fortunate–no need for Chicago's finest to intervene.

Well, as usual, my broker friend was right–tickets became

more affordable, as game time was closer at hand. Finally, at 6:15, the three of us bought our tickets. Since getting three tickets together was difficult, Patrick and his brother in law bought tickets in the 200 level, behind first base, for $1200—quite the deal. And I bought a ticket, nine rows behind home plate, for $2300—using a credit card, no less. This was quite a steal, compared to what that ticket was fetching only 24-48 hours beforehand—anywhere from $25,000 to $8000, depending on, exactly, where the box seat was located.

And, even more fun, my seat was a few rows behind where Eddie Vedder, lead singer of Pearl Jam, was sitting. Presumably, he got an even better deal for his ticket. Is free considered a deal? So, not only did I purchase my ticket for a relative bargain, I saw the Cubs win—3-2—their only win at home for the World Series. The game's highlight was a Kris Bryant home run that served as a catalyst for both winning the game and setting the stage for their trip to Cleveland for games six and seven.

You may now wonder if I travelled to Cleveland for the decisive game seven, after they won game six, 6-0. Nope, not this time—maybe the next time, if there is one. At this point, I can rest, peacefully, having seen all of my favorite Chicago sports teams win at least one game in their respective Championship games—what a special treat!

If I had attended game seven, it would have been quite the experience. The Cubs were leading by three runs going into the bottom of the eighth inning, when the Indians tied the game on a home run by Rajai Davis. After neither team scored in the ninth inning, the game went into extra innings, which were delayed by rain. This rain delay was a godsend, as it allowed the Cubs to collect themselves and score two runs in the top of the 10th. But, hold on, the Indians continued the battle in the bottom of the 10th, but scored only one run, stranding a runner, and eventually losing the game—on November 2, 2016, the Chicago Cubs were WORLD SERIES WINNERS—a first in 108 years! The Ricketts family delivered on their promise to bring Chicago a Cubs World Series Championship. Is it a bit presumptuous that my getting Tom and his family on the field, several years beforehand, had an effect on their buying the team—yeah, you're right, probably a little too presumptuous.

LESSON LEARNED:

In this case, especially, even when ticket demand is at historically high levels—70 plus years-worth—you can still get that elusive ticket to your favorite team's championship. BE PATIENT (as tough as this is)—you'll be the beneficiary. Keep tabs on ticket prices, get to the scene of the action to do some "market research" and then pounce within a short time before the game's starting time. It also would help if you have a friend who is a ticket broker and, actually, has your best interests at heart—this is almost as rare as a Cubs World Series appearance.

BEING UPGRADED

Part of the thrill and excitement, attending many of these events, has been enjoying them in a style that most typical spectators can only imagine–a style that befits the well connected, professionally, financially or personally (not really my style). As regaled in the aforementioned pages, I have been fortunate to experience VIP suites, media tents, corporate VIP tents, a members-only clubhouse of the world's most prestigious country club, press boxes, photographer's pit and various playing surfaces–ice, baseball field and basketball court. Most of these instances have occurred as a result of "acting like I belong" rather than "actually belonging." Either way, it may be of interest to describe, in greater detail, what it's like to be part of the VIP/media scene.

THE PRESS BOX

Not every press box is the same, of course, but there are some commonalities–for starters–they all have members of the media, who are pretty down to earth, generally, but do become a bit spoiled in their expectations of how they want to be treated–an interesting dichotomy. Nonetheless, they are affable enough, not terribly filtered with their comments, and enjoy a good laugh or story–not that they received that from me, over the years. As a matter of fact, they were usually exasperated from my usual stream of questions and lack of reporting capabilities.

First, when you're in the press box, you can count on an excellent, unobstructed view that also offers plenty of space and elbow room to do your work and be a responsible member of the media. There's no need to tell anyone "down in front"–you are the front, above the crowd.

Second, there are some magnificent spreads, which are supplied, affording the press with all the delectable nourishment they need to be informative, succinct, accurate and, of course, unbiased. Depending on the venue and the game, itself, the press box includes a wide assortment of foods and beverages–you can count on alcohol, too–beers and hard liquor, to get the creative juices flowing (like the liquids themselves). For sure you can count on other types of beverages–sodas, water, juices, etc. There is not a fully stocked bar, but believe me, you'll feel at home.

The foods themselves include pizza, hot dogs, burgers, chips, fries, etc. and plenty of desserts to complete the epicurean experience. You won't mistake the meals for a Four Seasons restaurant, but there is a distinct advantage over the Four Seasons–the spread (all of it) is free–on the house–leave your wallet at home. And, everything is in great abundance, constantly being replenished. Now you understand why some of today's finest media members are often standing sideways and rarely seen on the beach showing off their "enhanced" figures—sans clothing.

CORPORATE AND MEDIA TENTS AND SUITES (AND CLUBHOUSE)

Again, not every tent and suite is the same, but you can expect to have a more luxurious sporting experience than if you're in the press box. Depending on the event, the suite or tent may or may not offer any view of the action. Often, the suite or tent is where you go before, after or even during the event (if you find the action less interesting than indulging yourself in the waiting buffet). Here, you'll be treated to a little more white glove treatment, and have people waiting on you, catering to your every want and need. The array of beverages is close to a fully stocked bar, affording easy access to the road to inebriation—a state where these guests can be found to enjoy heartily. The foods, themselves (think shrimp, oysters, crab legs, steak, and the like) are closer to what you might find at your favorite Four Seasons, but to your good fortune, without Four Seasons prices—always a welcome treat!

WITH THE PLAYERS

Being on the field, at the World Series, on the ice, at the Stanley Cup Finals, or in the photographers pit on Center Court at Wimbledon, is where you begin to fully appreciate, up close and LIVE, what it's like to be a real professional athlete. The speed of the game (tennis) and size of the ice and baseball field, are larger than they appear from your seats or couch, when watching the game on television. You can only imagine the skill and strength necessary to compete at these levels. To set foot on the sporting stage is an unforgettable memory—you begin to fantasize, in your wildest dreams, performing in front of thousands of fans, cheering your name, hopefully–unless you're striking out or missing an open goal, which would be more like a nightmare. And, just standing next to the athlete, you are overwhelmed by their celebrity–and you remind yourself to "keep your day job."

RANKING THE EVENTS

The previous stories represent the very top sporting events in the world, from my perspective. My criteria is the following:

- The event has to involve either a Championship or a game showcasing the best players in the respective sport
- The event has to be considered prestigious and, accordingly, a very high ticket demand
- The event has to have been played for at least 50 years
- The event has to rank as the top event in its respective category–i.e.–Auto racing; Indianapolis 500 vs any other race or Horse racing; Kentucky Derby vs Preakness, Belmont, etc.

Absent from this list is the Pro Bowl (The NFL's so called all-star game), which is excluded because of the low participation rate of the players elected to play the game and rather mediocre attendance. Essentially, this is nothing but a superficial exhibition of players mailing it in with the same type of involvement from their fans.

Also missing are the French Open and Australian Open, both great tennis tournaments, but surely not holding the same prestige as Wimbledon and the US Open. Another missing event is the British Open, which, certainly, is a great tournament, but in most opinions, would be behind the Masters and the US Open in importance–this claim might be debated by golfers who live east of the Atlantic.

For racing fans, you will not see any inclusion of the Daytona 500, LeMans or Monaco Grand Prix. Part of the rationale is my parochial perception that these do not compare to the Indy 500, but, again, that could be debatable. Finally, The Tour de France is absent because I'm not sure how much true interest there is in biking, beside the recreational nature of the sport. Likely, you may have an event that should be included in this list, but for the time being, this will remain as my list of the most prestigious sporting events, from an American's perspective.

IMPERATIVE TO SEE

Heavyweight Championship Bout
The Masters
NBA Championship Finals
Olympics
Stanley Cup Final
Super Bowl
Wimbledon
World Cup Final
World Series

IMPORTANT TO SEE

College Bowl game/BCS Championship
Indianapolis 500
Kentucky Derby
Major League Baseball All-Star Game
NBA All-Star Game
NCAA Basketball Final Four
NHL All-Star game
Ryder Cup

CHECK THE BOX

PGA Championship
US Open Golf
US Open Tennis

Reflecting on all of these experiences, the biggest thrill is to witness, first-hand—LIVE—your favorite team winning its respective championship. As wonderful as it was to attend the Masters, Wimbledon, Olympics, etc., the ultimate moments were watching the Bears win their first Super Bowl, the Bulls win their first NBA Championship and the Blackhawks winning the Stanley Cup Final (in electrifying fashion). At some point in your life, hopefully, your favorite team will make it to the Championship game and have an opportunity to be the world champion. You should make every conceivable effort to be there, in person—if your team wins, you will have many treasured memories!

COST TO ATTEND

Naturally, a consideration one has to include in attending these special events is the expense—tickets, transportation, lodging, etc. Since witnessing these events has occurred over a 35-year period—almost two generations—what I have paid to experience the aforementioned games would pale in comparison to what the expenses would be today.

However, it is fair to say, there are ways to reduce the costs of seeing these events LIVE. Furthermore, when attending these events, there are a number of principles that became part of my game viewing mantra, which should be helpful in making your LIVE viewing experience a success. And here would be my suggestions:

1. Explore all options
   - Your professional contacts–company, clients, vendors
   - Your personal contacts–family and friends
   - Ticket scalpers
   - Ticket brokers
   - Online web sites–StubHub, Craigslist, etc.
   - Event lotteries
   - Ticket selling services–Ticketmaster, etc.
   - The team or respective league itself.

Since I have been going to these various events, I have utilized virtually all of the above options. Certainly, the goal is to pay face price for your ticket. This can be accomplished more often than you might think.

2. Make the effort and commitment–plan ahead

3. Be prepared to go solo–this will give you far more flexibility

4. Be a risk taker–have the courage to go to the event without a ticket in hand and finagle a way in with only an hour or so before game time

5. Look for the opportunity–to be upgraded and ALWAYS look the part and act like you belong! Don't be intimidated–ever!

6. Be respectful to everyone who may be in a position to give you access to areas typically limited to VIPs, press, etc.–these people also can appreciate a creative explanation as to why they should allow you into better seats, etc.–be innovative!

7. Remember your next job may bring opportunities
    to you that were not previously available—job-
    hopping does have its benefits (throughout the years,
    I was with seven firms—broadcasting and money
    management—that often times allowed me the
    opportunity, directly or indirectly, to experience these
    thrilling moments.)

Clearly, since experiencing my first major sporting
event—LIVE—I have spent a few bucks—thousands of
dollars to cover all of the costs to attend these many events,
which spanned five decades. What better way could I have
spent these dollars—enjoying higher quality wine, sipping
the best single malt scotch, savoring Dom Perignon on a
regular basis? Maybe, but my sports spectating moments
have given me many wonderful memories. Alternatively,
if I had upped my consumption of quality beverages, who
knows what memories I would have, except for hundreds
of throbbing headaches—I'll take the events over the
hangovers.

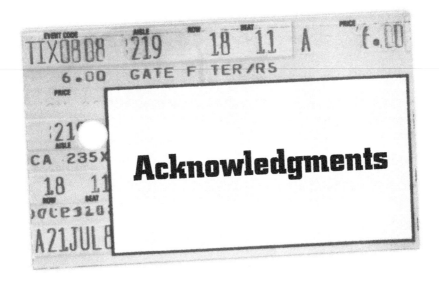

Acknowledgments

It's only appropriate that I give credit to a number of people who contributed to this writing. First, the person who introduced me to some of my early sporting events was my father. His background in broadcasting gave me access to many Chicago sporting events, particularly the White Sox and Blackhawks, while I was growing up. The events may not have been especially noteworthy, but they set the stage for my interest to enjoy more of them and in a bolder fashion, over the last 35 years.

Having developed a virtual obsession with attending these events all over the country and parts of the world, I was given permission to indulge myself with these junkets by my wife, Susan, who would carry on with the critical responsibility of keeping the household and kids in check, while I was gallivanting from one event to another.

Significantly, the person who actually suggested I publish my experiences as a sports spectator is Peter Kuhn, a Cleveland business associate. Formerly an executive of IMG, the sports agency organization, founded by Mark McCormick, Peter and I would meet over the years to discuss investment ideas, as he was responsible for managing a very wealthy family's estate, in recent years. During our meetings, he would relate some of his experiences as a sports agent in the 60s and 70s. While listening to his stories, I would share some of my own. Finally, after a number of story swapping sessions, Peter said, "Jeff, you have to write a book, from the typical sports fan's perspective, of attending these various events over the years–recounting the time, effort and process it required." I think he was saying, "If you can do it, anyone can."

For nearly 10 years, I have become friends with Ron Elberger, a prominent entertainment attorney, who represents David Letterman. He introduced me to Mickey Maurer, a highly successful entrepreneur, Pat Keiffner, the Publisher of IBJ Book Publishing (owned by Maurer), who is publishing my book, her team, Jodi Belcher, Production Manager, and Ashley Day, Lead Designer–I thank them for their guidance. Ron was gracious enough to read my manuscript and share his invaluable insights. In particular, his counsel regarding the usage of my photographed ticket stubs–their attendant organizational logos on the book's cover and back–was critical and prevented me from facing a few angry people in the NFL, MLB, NBA, etc. Who would think that one would need to receive the permission from these entities to print copies of tickets I possessed? Ron knew the licensing rights laws (which encompasses usage of tickets and their league/organization logos) very well and guided me through this circuitous process.

Also helping me with getting ticket stub usage approval were two other people–Rob Merrilees, a fellow Ravinia

Trustee, who was instrumental in my receiving the appropriate consent from the US Olympic Committee and George Vincent, a prominent Cincinnati attorney and minority owner of the Cincinnati Reds, who aided me with the permission from the MLB.

In closing, although I initially hesitated writing this book for fear that it would become a self-serving sports fan autobiography or, worse yet, a reading that would help cure people's sleeping disorders, hopefully, there are a few anecdotal nuggets that will motivate you to see the action LIVE, rather than from your couch.

So now that we come to the final sentence, (almost) and you are getting drowsy, I wish you a good night's sleep! (But, by all means, if you find yourself tossing and turning some future evening–keep my book handy–you'll be snoring in no time.)

About the Author

Raised in the northern suburbs of Chicago, Jeff graduated from both Loyola Academy and DePauw University and received his MBA from Loyola University.

Since that time, he was first a broadcasting professional, working primarily in radio. And for the last 30 years, he has managed financial assets for both institutional investors and high net worth individuals.

When not managing money, or attending sporting events, he has become actively involved with music. For many years, he was a member of The Recording Academy which produces the Grammy Awards shows. More recently, Jeff has served on the Board of Ravinia, a 100-year-old music venue, renowned as the summer home of the Chicago Symphony Orchestra and bringing top pop acts such as Bob Dylan, Paul Simon, Lady Gaga, Maroon 5, Sting, and many others to the Chicago music scene.

His poor attempt at humor was panned during one of his performances, years ago, at Second City, by his daughter, Courtney–8 years old at the time–who opined "the other guy on stage is much funnier than Dad."

At the end of the day, Jeff realizes how incredibly lucky he has been–first and foremost because of his loving family and, secondly, because of his many friends and business associates, who go back over 5 decades. Their supportive relationships with him are testimonials to the benefits of patience and tolerance (theirs)–for they will be rewarded with a left lane track to the pearly gates–hopefully, Jeff will not be far behind.